MW00928549

SPECTACULAR STORIES
FOR CURIOUS KIDS
SURVIVAL EDITION

Copyright ® 2022 Big Dreams Kids Books

Printed in the USA.

Book illustrations and cover design by Davor Ratkovic

Contents

10-Year-Old Punches
Alligator in the Face!

Sunny Florida is a wonderful place to swim and enjoy the warm days of Summer. 10-year-old Juliana Ossa was doing just that as she lazily swam along in the nice refreshing water of an Orlando park. Unknown to Juliana or her family, there was a 9-foot-long alligator in those waters with her. And this alligator thought that a 10-year-old girl might be a perfectly tasty snack.

Juliana had no idea it was there when it struck. It bit her in the leg. Can you imagine how scary that would be? I'll bet it really hurt, too. Juliana was one tough girl though. She started to punch it in the face, which seems like a very reasonable reaction. The problem was that this alligator didn't seem to mind it too much and wasn't letting go of her leg.

That's when Juliana remembered something that would save her life. Luckily, her family had once taken her to Gatorland, the theme park that is all about alligators. One thing you might learn there is that they're as old as dinosaurs. They've been around for millions of years. Another thing you might learn is what to do if you're attacked by one. Fortunately, not only did Juliana go there and learn this helpful piece of information, but she also remembered it when it mattered most.

Juliana had learned at Gatorland that if you stick your fingers up an alligator's nose when it's biting you, it can't breathe. So she did exactly that. She plugged up the alligator's nose with her fingers and waited. The waiting is the hard part. An alligator won't release you right away. It has to open its mouth so that it can breathe when its nose is plugged. This is your chance to escape. After waiting for a bit, Juliana was able to open its mouth and get her leg out. It worked! The alligator had run out of breath, so Juliana was then able to open its mouth.

She was only in 2 feet of water so she was able to jump up and start running away even with a hurt leg. Her step-uncle saw that she was in trouble and ran down to her and carried her the rest of the way out of the water. Juliana was bleeding pretty badly from where the bite had cut her leg and knee. An ambulance got there quickly and the paramedics were able to bandage her up. The paramedic said that Juliana was really tough about the whole thing. He also said that Juliana had told him that, "...if something is going to attack her, she has to attack back." I'll bet she doesn't get bullied much!

That's a great attitude when it comes to survival. Sometimes the correct move is to play dead if you're attacked by an animal such as a grizzly bear. But most of the time, the answer is to fight back in whatever way you can. It helps to know a few things like Juliana did about the animal that attacked her.

Keys to Survival: Juliana had to keep calm and not panic. That's REALLY hard to do! By not panicking, she was able to remember what she had learned about how to survive being bitten by an alligator. Plug up their nose and wait.

60 Hours at the Bottom of the Sea in a Bathroom?

The day had just started for Harrison Okene. He was on the *Jascon-4*, a tugboat in Nigeria that was on its way to rescue a massive oil tanker from a crazy storm. Harrison was the cook on this tugboat and he was used to being out at sea in terrifying weather.

Harrison had just woken up. It was 5 am. That's early. But the cook has to get up before a lot of the other sailors to get breakfast ready. He went to the bathroom. That's when it happened. Still in his underwear in the bathroom, a giant wave smashed into the side of the tugboat. The wave was so big that it knocked the tugboat on its side and cracked the boat nearly in half.

Poor Harrison was thrown out of the bathroom stall. The day was off to a pretty terrible start, but it would only get worse. Harrison ran through a hallway to get to the emergency hatch. Just as he was about to get there, water started rushing in and he was forced to run back the other way. The boat was filling up with water now. The water was cold, really cold. He ran into the captain's quarters and jumped into the little private bathroom that was just for the captain. That's when the *Jascon-4* flipped upside down as the waves continued to beat on it.

It's hard to imagine a scarier experience than this, but it kept getting worse. The boat began to sink. Harrison knew it was sinking, but he was trapped. There was nowhere for him to go. What would save his life was that he happened to get into the only place on the boat where there was some trapped air. There was around 4 feet of it to be exact. He had to tread water to keep his head in that air pocket as he felt the boat sinking. Harrison knew right when it finally hit the ocean floor. It probably took a little while to sink all the way to the bottom. Harrison must have felt like he was miles from the surface.

Amazingly though, he was still alive. There was something else in there that would help to save his life and was almost as important as the air. He found a can of coke. With nothing else to drink, this can would save him. On the ocean floor, at least the boat was no longer getting knocked around by the storm. All of that was still going on 100 feet above him. It was much quieter on the bottom of the ocean, and much darker. Everything was pitch black. Wearing just his underwear, Harrison was COLD. With the storm still raging, there was little hope for a rescue, but for some reason, Harrison decided that he wouldn't give up. He would do his best to keep going. He had nothing to eat. He only had a small pocket of air to breathe. Eventually, that air would run out.

As well as being both lucky and stubborn, Harrison was also quite clever. He swam through the darkness into the captain's quarters to try and grab things that might float which would help him tread water. This was not easy to do in the darkness but he managed to get lots of random pieces of wood to make a little raft to hang on to. This kept him from spending his energy treading water. But it didn't help with any of his other problems.

A whole day came and went. And then another, and another. Harrison knew he would be dead soon. His skin was in bad shape from being in salt water for 3 days. His tongue was swollen and that hurt. He was both starving and dying of thirst, and suffering from hypothermia as well because it was so cold. With no hope for rescue, it is incredible that anyone would make it as long as Harrison did.

That was when he heard it. A tapping noise. That was no fish. That was a person! He quickly swam into the bathroom below him and broke a faucet from the sink and started banging on the wall. Then he saw the beam from a flashlight! It's impressive that it didn't blind him after 3 days in complete darkness.

A team of divers had been called in to retrieve the bodies of the sailors who didn't survive the wreck. They sure didn't expect to find any survivors! One diver swam past and Harrison reached out to grab him. That diver must have gotten the shock of his life when he felt a hand grab him. Harrison had been in that bathroom for 62 hours. He likely only had a couple of hours of air left to breathe. He was saved just in time.

Harrison made a full recovery. And perhaps just as incredible, only 2 years later he got his certification for diving as a professional. He had promised God when he was down in that bathroom on the bottom of the ocean that he would never go near the water again if God saved him. He spent a lot of his time down there praying. He ended up changing his mind on that one and decided he wasn't done with the ocean after all. But Harrison swears that the only reason for his survival was his answered prayers to God for help. And the divers who saved him? They were there to give him his diploma when he graduated from diving school.

Keys to Survival: Harrison was able to find things in the captain's room by swimming around in the darkness. The can of coke and the wood that floated all helped to keep him alive. Nobody can tread water for 3 days. It was scary swimming around in the darkness to find stuff, but there are often things around that will help you. Be aware of your surroundings and use tools and other goods that may be helpful. Many would have given up after a day of that, but he hung on as long as he could. That is key to any survival situation.

An Arctic Survival Heroine

Ada Blackjack was familiar with the cold. She had grown up 40 miles north of Nome, Alaska. That put her right at the Arctic circle. She was Iñupiat, which were the indigenous people from that part of Alaska. You have to be tough to live in that part of the world and it's a good thing because Ada would need all of that toughness to survive the story you're about to read.

Ada wasn't raised by her parents so she wasn't taught the skills of her people. She didn't know how to hunt or fish. She didn't have any survival skills other than being used to the cold weather of her Alaskan home. She was raised by missionaries who taught her how to sew and cook. When her son was only 5 years old, Ada found herself in a situation where she was all alone in her remote wilderness home and running out of supplies. So what did Ada do? She walked and carried her son 40 miles to the little town of Nome. A 40-mile walk in that part of northern Alaska would not be fun no matter what time of year it was. She loved her son very much but didn't have enough money to give him a good life. She gave him to an orphanage so he could have shelter and food. She promised that she would do whatever it took to get him back.

That's one tough mom, and she meant her promise. They had just been through a nearly impossible ordeal together. It was only love and dedication that got them to Nome. After leaving her son with the orphanage she heard about a way to earn money. There was a team of explorers who needed someone from Alaska with sewing skills who also spoke English. This team was going to the uninhabited Wrangel Island which was nearly 600 miles from Nome. And those 600 miles were to the north. Yikes. The island was north of Siberia and these explorers wanted to go live on it so they could claim it for England since nobody lived there. Siberia isn't anywhere close to England and it's not clear that anyone else in England even knew about the island, much less wanted it to be a part of England.

Still, Ada needed money. She set off with the 4 young explorers, deep into the Arctic Circle. Ada had thought that she would be with a lot of her own people on this expedition but all of the other Iñupiat people ended up backing out. She was nervous about going alone with four men that she didn't know, but this job paid a lot of money. She was promised $50 a month which would have made her rich in the 1920s. She could think of no other way to get her son back, so she went. She got aboard the ship and they set sail for Wrangel Island. They were supposed to be there for a year. There were plenty of fish and wild game to catch and eat. Ada cooked and kept everyone's clothes sewn together.

But then summer ended. You can probably guess what happens after summer is over on an island that is north of Siberia. The ice moves in and the wild game becomes really hard to find. The food runs out. The team of 5, plus a cat named Victoria (or Vic for short), were supposed to be picked up by another boat. But either the boat set sail too late or the ice came early. The boat couldn't get through the ice. The explorers were on their own...until the next summer. They didn't have nearly enough food saved. As one of the men got sick with scurvy, the other 3 men decided to leave him with Ada and go get help by crossing the ice to Russia. Nobody ever saw them again.

Ada had to take the place of 3 men in taking care of the sick man left behind. She had to hunt, fish, get firewood, and be a doctor, as well. She had to do all of this through a winter in the Arctic. Oh, and their only shelter was heavy tents. This was an incredibly difficult task but she kept the man alive for 6 months. Unfortunately, he eventually died. She was then all alone, except for the cat. Even though the sick man had not helped her do anything, at least she wasn't all by herself trying to not be eaten by polar bears. (Wrangel Island has more than any place in the world!) The solitude didn't seem to bother Ada too much. She had a son to get back to. She learned how to shoot birds, catch foxes, and hunt seals. She did all of this in temperatures that were 50 degrees below zero. That's as cold as cold gets! In August of 1923, two years after getting to the island and after three months all by herself (other than the cat), a boat finally came for her.

The crew of the boat that "rescued" her were impressed. To them, it seemed that Ada was perfectly content and could have easily kept on living there. (They were also impressed with the cat.) She had mastered the art of arctic survival. She was reunited with her son. And even though she wasn't given as much money as she was promised, it was enough to take her son to Seattle where it wasn't nearly as cold as Wrangel Island.

Wrangel Island never did become a British territory as the explorers had hoped. That was just fine with Ada. She had never cared about that anyway. It was also just fine with all the polar bears who lived there. Maybe that's why the island was uninhabited by people in the first place?

Keys to Survival: Ada was an expert seamstress but not an expert hunter. She had to learn. She kept trying and refused to give up. That attitude is why she stayed alive. She was also able to skin animals and make warm clothes, as well as catch them for food.

76 Days Alone in the Atlantic

BOOM! What in the world? Steve Callahan groggily woke up in his 20-foot sailboat. And then he was wide awake. Freezing cold water was pouring over him. It had been storming during the night and he had finally fallen asleep. He had left the Canary Islands (off the coast of Morocco) a week ago. He was way out in the Atlantic. His boat shouldn't be running into things. But here he was in the middle of the night with a giant hole in his boat.

Steve had loved sailing as soon as he tried it in Boy Scouts. When he was just 12 years old, he was sailing so far out into the Atlantic Ocean that he couldn't see the land. When he was 16, he was regularly out by himself on his boat all day. He had wanted to sail by himself across the Atlantic ever since those early days sailing as a Boy Scout. Now he had done it. He had sailed from Rhode Island down to the Caribbean and then across to England.

He had all kinds of adventures and met interesting people. He entered a sailing race back to the Caribbean but his boat was damaged by a big storm. This was no big deal for Steve. He was an extremely experienced sailor. He just went to Spain to get his boat fixed. Once that was done, he headed back home. That was when disaster struck.

Maybe it was a giant shark or a huge whale that hit his boat. Those were the most likely culprits. But one thing was certain. Steve's boat was sinking and it was sinking fast. At first, he just thought that he was a goner, but then his survival instincts kicked into high gear and he got busy.

He inflated his 6-foot-long life raft. Even as his boat went below the frigid Atlantic water, he kept diving down into the darkness to grab what he could. It's a good thing he did. That would have been extremely scary. You can't see a thing, you're holding your breath, the water is freezing, and your boat is going down and you're swimming around in it. Terrifying! Steve bravely grabbed some much-needed supplies and made it safely to his life raft.

He was now bobbing up and down in the waves, 800 miles away from the islands that he had left a week earlier. That was a scary first night in the storm because he kept having to bail water out of his rubber raft with a tin can. But he had some food, a little water, and enough supplies to live for a couple of weeks, he thought. Little did he know, he would need to fight for MUCH longer than that.

He had a solar still which was really important. It would clean the salt out of the ocean water which would give Steve some drinkable water. He also had a spear gun for fishing. It was hard at first to figure out how the solar still worked. It had been on his boat for this exact situation. He had to take it apart to figure it out and after a couple of days, it started to work. It worked well enough to give him the equivalent of a bottle of water each day. That wasn't much, but it was enough to keep him alive.

After two weeks of living like that, he saw a boat! And there was one other thing that Steve had...a flare gun. He jumped up and fired it into the air. The ship never saw him and just kept on its merry way with no idea that it had just passed a man desperately fighting for his life.

Over the next couple of weeks, he saw more ships. There were around 7-9 ships that passed right by him, a couple that were less than a mile away. That's close out in the middle of the ocean. But not one of those ships ever saw him. Each time one passed by, it was soul-crushing. These missed chances would fill Steve with despair.

Being stuck in a 6-foot-long life raft is a terrible thing. Poor Steve was covered in saltwater sores. Being in salty water is bad for your skin and can make you extremely uncomfortable. He was also constantly on the brink of starving and always thirsty. Barnacles were growing on the bottom of his life raft which attracted small fish. This was much-needed food for Steve. But these fish also attracted sharks and they were aggressive.

After 40 days at sea, a fish ripped part of his raft. This made it even harder to stay above the water. Each time he tried to fix it with his arms in the water, the sharks would see their chance and come in close. Fortunately, he had an air pump with him but was constantly using it. Steve worked for 10 days to fix the raft but finally gave up. Not being able to fix the raft would mean that Steve wouldn't live for much longer. Luckily, he got really scared at the thought of dying, got back to work, and figured it out! He finally found a way to patch the raft and that accomplishment gave him so much joy that he had to keep going. Steve later said that "I found a way to fix the raft and it felt like the biggest victory of my life."

By this time, Steve had been drifting for 76 days. That's two and a half months where each day can kill you (each night, too). His solar still quit working and he only had a little water left. He was near the end. He said, "My body and mind were shutting down; it was as if I could feel all the people who had ever been lost at sea around me. I had no more to give."

And that's when he was finally found. Steve had drifted all the way across the Atlantic Ocean to the Caribbean. He didn't know it but he had floated more than 2,000 miles! That night he saw lights and they weren't boat lights. That was land! The next day, fishermen on a small boat saw birds flying all around his raft and went closer to investigate. The lights he had seen were on the island of Marie Galante which is just south of Guadeloupe. Steve had lost 40 pounds and wouldn't be able to walk for another 6 weeks. He was saved just in the nick of time.

Keys to Survival: Steve survived for 76 days by eating raw fish and birds that he caught with his spear gun. Similar to lots of our survivors, Steve saved his life by grabbing as many supplies as he could from his sinking boat when he had the chance. That takes quick thinking. One of the hardest things about surviving that long by yourself is that every day is the same. That can drive you crazy! Keeping a good attitude is one of the most difficult things to do in these situations, but also one of the most important. It keeps you fighting. That's what Steve did, working for more than a week to fix his life raft, working for days getting the solar still to work, and keeping his hopes up each time a ship would pass by without seeing him.

A 7-Year-Old Survived a
1720-Foot Megatsunami?

This story is about the legendary megatsunami of 1958. It's the biggest wave in modern history and we've known some big waves. This is the biggest of them all. Just to give you some context, the destructive tsunami that hit Japan in 2011 was 133 feet tall. That's taller than a 10-story building!

The deadliest tsunami of all time happened in 2004. It was 167 feet tall and damaged all of Indonesia. It was so damaging because it struck a part of the world where lots of people lived. A 167-foot wave is really scary. That's taller than a 15-story building. But what happened in 1958 made a wave that was an unbelievable 1720 feet tall. That's nearly 300 feet taller than the 102-story Empire State building which was once the tallest building in the world.

Can you imagine a wave hitting New York City that was taller than the Empire State building? It doesn't seem possible. Luckily, this happened away from where there were lots of people. It happened all the way up in Alaska in Lituya Bay. But there were *some* people around.

There were some fishing boats anchored in the bay. One boat was called the Edrie, and it was 40 feet long. On this boat was a 7-year-old boy, Sonny.

Sonny was out fishing with his dad, Howard, who was a professional fisherman. They rode into the bay at 8:00 in the evening. They anchored and went to bed.

That's when the earthquake started. Even though Howard and Sonny were on a boat, they could still feel it. They had already fallen asleep but all the shaking woke them up. It was a big earthquake that measured 7.8 on the Richter Scale. That's big. It was a little after 10 pm. The sun sets late that far north in the summer. The sun was just setting and it was still a little light out.

They heard something that sounded like an explosion. The earthquake caused a massive rock slide. People 50 miles away heard it! So for Sonny and Howard, it was REALLY loud. 90 million tons of rocks crashed down 3,000 feet into the bay. This was not good. What happened next was the wave.

Lituya Bay is 720 feet deep. How could a wave be twice as high as the depth of the water? All of that rock crashing with so much force into the water, created the biggest wave that any person has ever seen. Howard didn't have enough time to pull up the anchor. As soon as he saw the wave, he only had seconds to get ready, but what he did next, saved their lives.

He couldn't pull up the anchor but let out the anchor chain as deep as it would go and started the motor of the boat. The water that Howard and Sonny were in was perfectly still. When the wave got to them, it was a 100-foot wall of fast-moving water that would only get bigger. Howard pointed the boat at the wave.

He thought it was certain death. But he threw a life preserver at Sonny and told him to start praying.

Amazingly, the boat started to climb the wave and the anchor chain snapped which freed them. Howard gave the engine all the throttle he could for maximum power. The giant wave carried them over land and trees. Howard thought that they would crash onto the trees at any moment. Luckily for Howard and Sonny, the Edrie did not fall back down with the massive wave. Instead, they made it over the crest of the wave (hundreds of feet in the air) and were able to ride the backside of the wave back down into the bay instead of heading into the land with the wave.

After the main wave passed, they weren't out of danger. The water level of the bay had returned to normal but was filled with 20-foot waves just bobbing up and down. Howard still had to work hard to keep the boat upright for another 30 minutes until the bay calmed down. Then he calmly motored out of the bay. Another boat that had been in the bay was dumped on top of some trees after "surfing" the megatsunami with the front of the boat facing away from the wave...miraculously, the man and wife on that boat lived as well.

The wave had been so big that it ripped down trees that had been 700 feet above the bay on the mountains around it. Despite this experience, Sonny didn't move away from the ocean. He even joined the Navy. After his service, he moved back to Alaska and raised a family.

Keys to Survival: Sonny's prayer may have helped, but if you're on a boat and you see a big wave coming, you want to point the boat right at the wave. If the wave hits you sideways, the boat will roll. If you face it head-on, you might be able to make it over the wave while keeping your boat from flipping over as Sonny and Howard did. Even though Howard couldn't release the anchor, letting out the line as far as it could go allowed the boat to rise with the force needed to break the chain. If the chain hadn't broken, the boat would have been pulled underwater. The Ulrichs were extremely lucky, but they did everything they could to give themselves the best chance to survive.

Jaguars, Alligators, and Anacondas, Oh My!

Antonio Sena's mind filled with terror and dread. The engine of his small prop plane had just died. The little Cessna plane was almost 50 years old. It had been risky to fly it, but Antonio had a job to do. He was 3,000 feet in the air over the Amazon rainforest. He was in the middle of nowhere. There is never a good place for something like this to happen to a pilot. But there are extremely bad places for it to happen and the remote jungle is one of those places.

It was now eerily silent so high in the air without the noise of the engine running. There was only the sound of the wind. If being 3,000 feet in the air in a plane with a dead engine isn't dangerous enough, there was also Antonio's cargo. He was carrying nothing but diesel fuel, 160 gallons of it. That meant that he was basically on a flying bomb that was about to fall into the jungle. He was taking the fuel to miners in one of the most remote regions of Brazil. He figured that he had maybe 5 minutes before he crashed. He needed to find the best spot to land and he needed to find it NOW.

That's when he saw them. Palm trees. All that was below him were trees (this was the rainforest after all) but palm trees only grow near water, such as lakes or rivers, in the rainforest. Antonio would not stand much of a chance if he crashed into a bunch of trees, but if he could find a little opening...

So he aimed the plane (which was starting to fall pretty fast at this point) toward the palm trees in the hopes that he might find an opening to some water below the giant canopy of trees. WHACK! The top of a palm tree hit the plane. And then another, WHACK! And then there were lots of trees hitting the bottom of the plane and it got really loud and scary.

The next thing Antonio knew, his plane was on the ground...and he was still alive! There was metal all over him and he realized that he was completely drenched in gasoline. Not good. He knew he didn't have much time. Fortunately, the windshield of the plane was broken and gone. Wisely, he quickly grabbed what he could and got out of the plane. It was only a moment later that the plane exploded.

Phew! He had made it this far and amazingly had no broken bones or bad injuries. That might have been a miracle right there. That was pretty much where the good news ended. Antonio was hundreds of miles from a town and there are a lot of scary things that live in the Amazon...things like giant anaconda snakes, jaguars, alligators, and big poisonous spiders. This was not the best place for a casual stroll. He had done well to grab some things before he scrambled out of the plane. He had managed to grab several bottles of water and soft drinks, a lighter, two pocket knives, a rope, a flashlight, and a bag of bread. He also had a cell phone with no signal but lots of battery life and his wristwatch. Not bad! He could work with that.

Antonio stayed close to the crash site in the hopes that rescue planes would see it. That was a good plan. The search planes were out looking for him when he didn't show up with his delivery. But Brazil has 1.8 million square miles of rainforest. People go missing all the time. Most are never found. Antonio stayed near the crash site for 5 days. That was when he heard it. It was a plane! He yelled and screamed. It passed right over him. They never saw him through the dense canopy of trees. His heart sank as the sound of the plane got further and further away. It was just too hard to see a crashed plane in this jungle. He was done waiting.

Antonio now knew that he was on his own and that he would have to save himself. He collected his things and began to walk. He didn't get very far. The Amazon can be extremely thick and dense. It's not so easy to walk through a jungle. He went back to the crash site as night fell, not sure how he was going to survive this. That's when he started talking to God for the first time since he had been a young boy. He just wanted to see his family again. He was hungry, tired, and scared. He had been in the Amazon, alone for 8 days. But now he was determined to make it. He felt that he had God on his side.

He pushed through the dense jungle, cutting away at it with only his pocket knives. He encountered spider monkeys who threw branches at him and destroyed his shelters. He got into a routine. From the first light of morning to noon, he hiked and cut his way through the jungle. This was exhausting work. In the 3 hours from noon to 3, he worked on finding a good place to spend the night. He always tried to spend the nights up on a hill, not close to any streams or rivers. Predators caught their meals near the water. Antonio knew that he couldn't sleep near the river. That would be much too dangerous. Anacondas, jaguars, and alligators knew that their prey needed water so that's where they hunted.

In the next two hours of the day, he would build his shelter, and then he would work on getting a fire going. Thanks to his wristwatch, he could keep the same schedule every day. But eventually, his body began to break down. After fighting his way through the jungle for four weeks, he was struggling. He had lost 55 pounds and Antonio wasn't a hefty guy to begin with. It was getting harder and harder to keep going.

He ate the same fruit that he saw monkeys eating. Maybe that's why they liked to throw things at him. He ate eggs he found, but it was never enough. Antonio was slowly starving to death. On the morning of his 36th day in the jungle, he told God that he was giving up. He had gone as far as he could, but he managed to get moving that day anyway. After a few hours of his usual trudging through the jungle, he saw it. He hadn't seen the color white in 36 days. That wasn't a color that you saw in the Amazon. He walked toward it.

Antonio kept expecting it to disappear but as he got close enough to touch it, he realized that it was a tarp. Not only that but there were tools and a bucket full of nut shells. Then he heard something. It was a man scavenging for nuts. Another human! Antonio introduced himself and explained his situation. Antonio desperately needed something to eat. The nuts tasted glorious.

There was a family of people there collecting nuts. They had not been in that part of the Amazon in 3 years. It wasn't usually where they went. They did everything they could to help the jungle castaway and radioed for help.

Antonio's family had never given up on him. His brother and sister worked tirelessly to find him and manage the search effort. They had gotten lots of false leads by this point and couldn't hear the nut collectors well through the phone. They asked a question that only Antonio would know the answer to. What was the name of his brother's dog? They faintly heard the weak voice of Antonio answer, "Gancho." Antonio's brother screamed in joy. His brother was alive.

The family of nut collectors refused to accept any kind of reward for finding Antonio. A police helicopter carried Antonio back to the waiting arms of his brother and sister. Through all the tears, Antonio managed to say, "I did this for you. I survived for you." Antonio's story captured the hearts of all Brazilians. 2021 had been an awful year in Brazil because of the Covid-19 pandemic. Hundreds of thousands of people died there.

This made Antonio's amazing survival story the first piece of really good news that a lot of people had heard in quite some time. His survival became something of a national symbol of hope. The key to survival tends to include being strong enough to just keep going! That is what kept Antonio alive. Motivated by the love he had for his family, he kept going.

Keys to Survival: Antonio's quick thinking when he grabbed a bunch of things from the plane was really smart. It was also smart to know that he had to get out of the plane as fast as he could. It's always a good idea to wait by your crash site. It is easier for rescuers to see the wreckage of a plane, boat, or car than it is to see a person. If they can't see the wreckage, which was the case for Antonio, you have to get moving. The key for Antonio was staying away from predators by sleeping away from streams and rivers. He also ate the berries that the monkeys ate. This kept him from accidentally eating something poisonous. The main key was that he refused to give up, which is often the hardest thing to do.

Happy Thoughts & Rainwater
Are Sometimes All You Need

These sisters are so cute. They're lucky for a lot of reasons. For one, they live on a beautiful 80-acre property in northern California. And two, they had learned lots of survival tips from their parents and they enjoyed TV shows about survival. Nobody thought that they would need to use what they had learned.

Leia Carrico was 8 years old. Her sister, Caroline was just 5. But they were as tough as they were cute. They asked their mom if they could go for a quick hike by themselves. The Carricos are a hiking family. The girls had been out lots of times. So their mom wasn't worried about a quick hike in the middle of the day.

Unfortunately, the girls got lost. They realized they were walking around in circles when they saw the same metal poles that they had already walked past once. Even though they were in trouble, the young girls started making some good decisions.

It was early March and temperatures can drop during the night in northern California. Not only was it cold that night, but it started to rain as well. This was a really bad combination and Leia and Caroline's parents knew it. When the girls didn't return, they were frantic and called in help. The sheriff's department gathered 250 people along with two helicopters and sent them searching for the girls.

The girls had seemingly vanished. If the girls had gotten wet with the temperature dropping, they could have gotten hypothermia which would have been dangerous. Leia draped her jacket over a bush and they huddled together for warmth underneath it. This kept them dry which probably saved their lives. They also drank rainwater off of the leaves. They were quite hungry but they couldn't do anything about that.

That night Caroline was very scared and couldn't stop crying. That's very understandable since she was only 5 years old. Leia told her sister to keep thinking happy thoughts. She kept Caroline from losing faith that their parents would find them. Leia also stayed awake as much as she could through the night in case animals came close. There are black bears in that area and even more dangerous...mountain lions.

Even though Caroline was only 5, she remembered the lessons from the survival TV shows she watched with her sister. She remembered that one of the most important things to do when you're lost is to stay in one place. That makes it easier to be found and rescued. So that's what the sisters did. They stayed right there even though they had to wait another entire day and make it through another scary night in the woods.

Finally, on that 3rd day, they heard voices calling their names. They yelled out to answer and two very excited firefighters walked out of the woods. The rescuers said that the girls looked great, as if they had just left for a short walk. They didn't look at all like they had just spent two nights by themselves in the woods. It was an extremely emotional reunion with their parents. Their parents had been terrified and were overjoyed to see the girls.

They were taken to the hospital and fed lots and lots of pizza. Their mom said that it would be a while before they went for a hike by themselves again and that when they did, they would have GPS trackers on them so she would know exactly where they were at all times. She added "I'm trying not to punish them. They saved each other. I'm the proud mom. I raised superheroes."

Keys to Survival: The girls stayed in one place when they realized they were lost. Lots of times, you can only get more lost if you keep moving. They also did everything they could to keep their spirits up and stay positive. One of the main things that helped was being able to stay dry through the rain and the cold. Covering a bush with a rain jacket and sleeping under that bush saved them. They were lucky to have rainwater to drink. The girls made many good decisions during their ordeal.

Kids Riding Tornados

The Wizard of Oz is a famous movie that was made in 1939. Dorothy is the girl who is the main character and in the story, she is picked up by a tornado and carried off to the fictional land of Oz. A few years later, in 1955, a 9-year-old really did go for a ride in a tornado! But first she rode a horse.

There's not a whole lot around Bowdle, South Dakota. It's a very rural part of the state. Sharon Weron was 9 years old and riding a horse home from a neighbor's house. Her mom was following in her car and saw everything.

Just as Sharon and her horse reached their house, the tornado was on them. They had very little warning. Sharon's mom saw the tornado pick up her daughter (and horse), spin them around wildly, and carry them away. Sharon was wearing a blue shirt so her mom was looking for that in the tornado and could see her spinning. The tornado carried them around 1,000 feet, over several fences, and dumped Sharon in a ditch.

She was wearing a leather jacket and pulled that up around her head during her flight. There was hail and all kinds of debris flying around inside the tornado with her. Sharon's hands were badly bruised from being hit by the hail and who knows what else. She remembered hitting the ground and grabbing the grass so that she wouldn't get sucked up again.

As she looked around, she found her horse. He was just standing there not far from her. Both were a little beaten up but okay. That's crazy, right? Their story got picked up by newspapers and spread all over the world. Reporters had no reason to doubt the story. As unbelievable as it seems, it still holds up as credible. Sharon's ride was also witnessed by neighbors. The Guinness book of world records listed Sharon's ride as the furthest anyone had ever ridden in a tornado until 2006. It's remarkable that both Sharon and her horse lived through such a terrifying experience. That has to be the craziest horse story in the history of the world!

So what happened in 2006? That story lends further credibility to Sharon's story. Matt Suter was staying with his grandmother in Fordland, Missouri. Matt was 19 years old. The storm was getting bad. As Matt tried to lock the windows in his grandmother's mobile home, the windows were ripped away and carried off into the EF2 tornado. The walls were sucked up too. And with them, went poor Matt.

He was pulled up and up, so high that he couldn't breathe. He couldn't see much of anything and passed out. There's no telling how high he got. Incredibly, he woke up in a grassy field and he was okay! He had no broken bones and even felt fine. He was more than 1300 feet from where the tornado lifted him up. This is still the current record for the distance a person has flown inside a tornado.

Neither Sharon (or her horse) or Matt had flown in an airplane before flying in a tornado. But they all flew further than the Wright Brothers did on their historic first flight on an airplane. That's a remarkable feat. Not everyone is so lucky. Tornadoes are often fatal. The fact that these tornado riders lived to talk about it, makes their stories truly amazing.

Keys to Survival: The best way to live through a tornado is not to go riding in it. You want to take shelter in a basement or interior room. It's best if there are no windows in the room. Underneath stairs is a good place to hide, as well. While taking shelter, it's a good idea to cover yourself with a mattress if you can get one, to protect you from anything that might fall on you. Some tornado warning signs are a green sky, really big falling hail, and a loud roaring sound like a train. You're nearly out of time if you hear that!

Trapped 2,000 Feet Below the Surface of the Earth

The men had all gone to work that morning as if it were any other day. It WAS like any other day...until it wasn't. These men were miners. They were mining for copper and gold in the San Jose mine in northern Chile in South America. Mining can be an extremely risky business. The conditions are often hazardous and you need to be either very brave or a little nuts to do it.

As the men went about their business down there, they heard a gigantic explosion above them. It sounded as if the world was ending. A massive chunk of rock had come loose from the mountain above the mine. This chunk was the size of a 45-story building. It was 550 feet high and weighed nearly 800,000 tons. That's a big chunk of rock! The statue of liberty only weighs 27,000 tons. That's like 30 Statues of Liberty crashing their way through the mine.

The San Jose mine had a road that went around and around deeper into the earth like a spiral staircase. The giant rock chunk crushed it all and brought down more of the mountain on top of it as it fell. But amazingly, the 33 miners that were at the bottom of the mine were not crushed. They were all alive. But their situation was not good when the shaking stopped and they all got back up off the ground. They didn't know it yet, but they were hopelessly trapped.

Most of the 33 miners figured that they would be rescued quickly. There was a steel room down at the bottom of the mine that was the size of a school classroom. There was some food in it for just this sort of emergency. They had 93 little cookie packages, 18 cans filled with tuna, a can of peas, a can of peaches, a can of salmon, and some milk (most of which was spoiled). That's not much for 33 guys, but they wouldn't be in there for too long, right?

The most important thing was water for all of the men. There were only 10 bottles in the room. Fortunately, there was lots of stored water down there to keep the machine engines cool. It was dirty but drinkable. They figured that they couldn't eat much of the food, just in case they weren't rescued for a while. This was smart. Even though they were still hopeful, they ate as if they were planning for the worst-case scenario. Each day they would line up little cups and put one little teaspoon of tuna in each cup. Then they would add some water and stir it. They also each got two cookies to go with it. That was their one meal per day.

To have 33 men agree to that and stick with it as long as the Chilean miners had to is a pretty amazing achievement. Even though the miners were hopeful at first, the rescue miners at the top of the mine were not. After the crash, they had gone down as far as they could and ran into the giant chunk of rock. There was no getting around it. They figured that their friends at the bottom had to be dead.

The country of Chile started trying to drill through the massive piece of stone. News of the mine collapse spread all around the world and many countries sent big drills and machines to help. With each day that passed, the men got hungrier and hungrier. They started handing out 2 cookies every two days instead of every day. They were starving but kept their spirits up as best they could. They could hear drills far up above them but day after day, nothing ever broke through to where they were. They had some flashlights but they had no way to talk to anyone on the surface to let them know they were okay.

Finally, after two weeks of drilling, the men heard a drill getting close. Then it broke through! The men celebrated wildly and tied notes to the end of the drill to let the drillers know that they had found them. People couldn't believe that the men were still alive. There was now a small hole for the rescuers to pass food down and a telephone line so that they could communicate. Chile rejoiced when the news broke that all 33 men were still alive. But then the rescuers gave the miners the bad news that it would be months before they could safely drill a hole big enough and long enough to get the men out.

Can you imagine what it would be like to live mostly in darkness in such a small space for months and months with 32 other people? It had gotten incredibly stinky in just the first two weeks down there. But they had gotten past the truly difficult part. They were no longer starving and had cleaner water to drink now that rescuers knew they were still alive. They now had to somehow survive waiting with all of those different personalities and opinions. They made their own games with a handmade checkerboard and dominoes. They had prayer meetings. But it was not easy passing the time.

Days turned into weeks and weeks turned into months as the rescuers kept widening the hole. All of this was happening as the giant chunk of rock was shifting slightly with the drilling. It was an unstable and dangerous rescue effort. But on the 69th day of their ordeal, the first man was pulled up 2,000 feet through a tube in the rock. It took 30 minutes for each man to get pulled up inside a little capsule made of metal. News crews from all over the world were there along with Chile's president and all the excited families. It had to be incredibly disorienting for the miners to go from the stinky dungeon they had been living in to the party-like atmosphere on the surface. But their first bath in two and half months had to feel amazing! People celebrated this remarkable rescue all over the world.

Keys to Survival: What makes this story so spectacular is the cooperation of the 33 miners in such a difficult survival situation. They didn't expect to be stuck for so long but rationed their food anyway. 33 portions is a lot to separate out. That kept them from starving for the time it took rescuers to reach them and get them more supplies. After that, it was a matter of mental survival. Keeping a good attitude in these kinds of conditions is challenging. They stuck together as best they could to live for so long below the surface of the earth.

I've Got to Save My Dog!

It occurred to Jaime Rios that this might be the last day of his life. Water filled his truck as it sank into the canal in the darkness of that November night. As he fought to survive, he had the panicked thought that his dog must be doing the same thing.

Jaime was a duck hunter and had been looking forward to spending the day before Thanksgiving doing what he loved. He had chosen his 5-year-old chocolate lab, Stormy, as his partner for the trip. Jaime lived in California, not far from Sacramento. It was after midnight and they were headed for the duck blind. They had left early so that they could be in prime position first thing in the morning.

On the way, Jaime stopped for gas and headed inside. But before he did, he locked Stormy inside the bed of his truck under the camper shell. He had been in the habit of doing that because he had once met a man whose dog had been stolen out of the back of his truck. He loved his dogs and didn't want to lose them.

Soon after he got back out onto the highway, the fog started to get thicker. He was getting near the marsh that he was planning on hunting in. The marsh waters were warmer than the air which created the fog. A curve snuck up on Jaime through the fog and he hit it traveling too fast. His truck careened wildly as he fought to get it back under control. Gravity won and he found himself sliding backward down a steep embankment. He didn't know it yet, but the possibility of cold death waited at the bottom in the form of a deep canal with a strong current.

The truck splashed into the water and all of Jaime's lights went out. It all happened so fast. Jamie was struck by how serene and weird it was just floating down the canal inside his truck. Then he thought, "I sure hope this water isn't deep." It was. As his truck spins around, lazily floating downstream, Jaime jumps into action. He knows the truck won't stay afloat for long. The problem is that his doors are locked. The only way out is to break out.

He thinks about what he has that might break through a window. Amazingly, he had a glass breaker in the truck's console! It was made for just this kind of life or death situation and it had been in there for years. It had been a gift from a magazine subscription. Thank goodness! Breaking out of your car window isn't so easy, even if you have a glass breaker.

The tool wasn't that big and with his first swing... nothing. Uh oh. He swings it with both hands and it still just bounces off the glass harmlessly. Now he feels the water at his feet. He needs to get out of this truck and he needs out now. He climbs into the back seat to see if the back windows are any easier to break. They aren't. So he lies back and kicks the window with both feet. Still nothing. The water keeps rising inside the truck. It's now over the seat. He keeps kicking until the water is above his head.

He tries to dive down to his toolbox for something that he might have better luck with. As he does, the cold water swirls all around him. He has to go back up for air. There's not as much air up there this time, water has nearly filled the truck. He dives back down and has no luck with the toolbox but happens to touch a fire extinguisher. Could that help? With little time left, Jaime is willing to try anything.

He swings and swings the extinguisher and still has no luck breaking a window. He's nearly overcome with panic at this point. Why won't these stupid windows break?!? He's having to swing through all of the water which slows down his swings. Jaime's life passes in front of him. He sees it all but he doesn't have time for this. All he can think to do is to beg God for help. Nothing he has tried has worked, it might be in God's hands at this point. And right after he does, he hears a response in his mind. "You have a little more time. What will you do with it?" He notices that the water has stopped rising with just 2 inches of air in his truck. He responds, "I'm going to try a little harder."

He gulps breaths of air and goes down to pound the window with the fire extinguisher some more. He hits the window as hard as he can before getting more air. Then he repeats his efforts again and again. It feels to Jaime as if he does this forever but he keeps at it. It's pitch dark and the water is freezing. He's not getting anywhere and giving up crosses his mind. But then he remembers Stormy. He has to save her.

He keeps going, pounding the window for several more minutes. Then...what's this? It's a hole! He did it! Jaime quickly knocks the rest of the window out. He's finally free. But his job isn't done. He swims out to the tailgate and nearly panics when he realizes that it's locked. All he can do is try to rip it open out of sheer desperation. Afterward, Jaime would say that his desperation must have given him strength that he didn't ordinarily have. He's able to get his fingers under the camper shell and plants his feet against the truck. He pulls with every ounce of his strength and whatever extra strength he had in that moment. He couldn't swim out of there without Stormy.

Miraculously, the shell breaks apart and there's Stormy and she's okay! The two of them swim away from the truck to the embankment. But it's wet concrete with a steep slope. Jaime can't get up. He swims back to the truck and climbs on top to save energy. Stormy makes it out of the canal but comes back to Jaime. He didn't leave her and she won't leave him. Jaime pulls her up on top with him and notices how messed up his hand is. There's a huge hole in it! The stupid glass breaker had punctured his hand all the way down to the bone. He can't feel or move his fingers. He hadn't felt a thing when it happened, but now it was really starting to hurt.

Jaime swims back over to the bank again but still can't get up. He goes back to the top of the truck and thinks things through. He's still surrounded by fog. It occurs to him that there must be a ladder built into the concrete *somewhere*. He can't see very far in the darkness and the fog. His heart sinks as he realizes that he's going to have to wait for daylight. This is going to be a long night. He's soaking wet and it's really, really cold.

Hours pass. Jaime shivers through the longest night of his life. Stormy stays by his side. The two huddle together and her warmth probably saves his life. After around 3 hours, the sun finally makes an appearance. Thank goodness! The fog starts to lift as well. Things are looking up. About half a football field downstream, Jaime sees what looks like a ladder in the concrete. Not too far beyond that is a big pipe that the canal runs into. Upstream, there looks to be another ladder. It's a little further than the one downstream and it's against the current. He'll also be swimming against the wind going upstream. Jaime feels that he only has one swim in him. He's exhausted, injured, and probably slightly hypothermic. It's going to be extremely hard to force himself back into that freezing water. He has to be certain. He makes himself wait to be completely sure.

He notices some birds hopping around what he thinks is the upstream ladder. "Give me a sign... please!" Just then, one of the birds lands on what must be a ladder rung. That's the sign Jaime needed. Now for the most important swim of his life. It's entirely possible that he could plunge into the water and cramp up right away and drown. This is still an extremely dangerous situation.

Jaime can hardly breathe, the water is so cold but he gives it all he's got. By the time he and Stormy get to the ladder, he's too exhausted to lift his arm out of the water. Fortunately, there are rungs beneath the water. He's made it. He tells Stormy to wait so she doesn't get hit by a car and she obeys. Then on his way to the road, he walks past the spot downstream that he thought was a ladder. He gasps as he realizes that there is no ladder there after all. Swimming that way, he realizes, would have meant certain death. He would have gotten sucked into the pipe and drowned. Stormy might have as well. Jaime still had work to do. Fortunately, it didn't take long to get help. Before long, he and Stormy were in an ambulance. God, the birds, and Stormy, along with his good decisions and determination, had all saved his life. Jaime was one lucky guy that morning.

Keys to Survival: It's much harder to break out of a sinking car than most people realize. Jaime had to stick with it and keep fighting. It can be really difficult in any survival situation to stay determined. Giving up is much easier. He was able to avoid panicking which kept him on task. Jaime was also really smart to wait on top of his car instead of frantically trying to crawl out of the canal. Sometimes it is best to take your time and make the absolute best decision instead of rushing. That is really hard to do when you're cold, hungry, or hurting as Jaime was when he waited for daylight. That mindset also saved his life when he waited for proof that what he was seeing was actually a ladder. If he had made the easier choice to swim downstream, there is little doubt that he would have died.

Left for Dead, Travels 200 Miles for Revenge!

The fierce grizzly must have stood at least 12 feet tall. And in that powerfully massive body with deadly teeth and long lethal claws, was the drive to protect... and to kill. A man had startled her and she had two babies to protect. That man was in big, BIG trouble.

There might not be much that is scarier in the wilderness than an angry momma grizzly bear. That's exactly what explorer Hugh Glass accidentally ran into as he was hunting in South Dakota. He hadn't seen them in the brush. As she charged, he fired a bullet right into her chest to save his life. It didn't seem to faze the bear at all. She attacked by sinking her teeth into Hugh's chest and picked him up and shook him. She picked him up several times with her jaws and threw him back down.

Hugh's gun was now too far away to help, but he fought bravely with his hunting knife. It was a life or death struggle and he managed to stay alive long enough for the rest of his men to get there and rescue him from the bear. He was alive, but barely. He had deep gashes and wounds all over his body (even his face, head, and neck) and lost a lot of blood. Who was this guy?

Hugh was born in Pennsylvania in the late 1700s. Before he was even 18 years old, he became a sailor in the Gulf of Mexico, and later became a pirate. Hugh ended up in Texas, which was a dangerous place in the early 1800s. Hugh was eventually captured there by the Pawnee people. The Pawnee would usually kill their captives but the chief liked this new guy and let him stay around.

Hugh lived as a Pawnee for 4 years and even got married. He learned a lot about how to survive and live as a Native American. Hugh got the chance to make a lot of money on an expedition for furs. It was dangerous work. 100 men signed up. They traveled over 1000 miles up the Missouri River to South Dakota where they fought with the Arikara tribe. Hugh's party was still being stalked and hunted by the Arikara when he surprised the Grizzly bear. The men he was with made a stretcher for him out of branches and carried him for three days.

Carrying Hugh this way slowed them down and they needed to get out of Arikara territory. Hugh was so badly injured that he couldn't walk or even talk. The men hadn't expected him to live for so long and they had carried him so far. Not only were they in hostile Arikara territory, but winter was coming. They needed to pick up the pace and they wouldn't be able to make it while carrying Hugh along. So the leader offered to pay two men to stay with him while he died and then bury him. One man was John Fitzgerald and the other was a young kid, Jim Bridger.

The two men stayed with Hugh for a few days until he developed a fever. He was in really rough shape. John had gotten really nervous about the three of them being stuck in Arikara territory and was getting more and more anxious to get somewhere safer. Hugh was dying anyway and nobody would know that they didn't bury him like they were supposed to. They took Hugh's gun, his knife, and anything useful that he had and set off to catch up with the rest of the men.

So there was Hugh with no supplies, not even a knife. His throat had been badly clawed by the bear so it was difficult to swallow food. He was able to eat some berries after his fever broke. He crawled down to the river for water. A rattlesnake approached him and he managed to kill it with a rock and eat that, too. That's when he decided that he would get revenge on the two men who left him for dead. Revenge wouldn't be easy! He was still hurt so badly that he couldn't even walk. Many of the survivors in this book were motivated by their loved ones. Not Hugh. The *only* reason he wanted to survive was the chance to get revenge on the men who had abandoned him!

He decided that the way to do that was not to follow them west but to crawl the 200 miles back to Fort Kiowa, the other way and get supplies. His wounds were so bad that his rib bones were showing. He also had a broken leg. Weeks after crawling all day and surviving on berries and river water with the occasional rotten meat from a wolf kill, he came across a pack of wolves with a fresh kill. It was a buffalo. That night he started a fire and made a torch. He crawled toward the wolves and amazingly scared them off with his torch. He stayed there for several days getting his strength back and drying some of the meat. It was then that he set his leg by tying branches around it for support and got well enough to limp instead of crawl. This was one tough guy!

Eventually, a band of friendly Sioux people found him and helped clean his infected wounds. They also took him the rest of the way to Fort Kiowa. It had been 6 weeks since the bear attack. There at the fort, he was able to get a gun and new clothes. He was now ready for the next part of his revenge plan. He headed for Yellowstone where he expected to find them. He caught a ride with some canoe ferriers and traveled with them for another 6 weeks.

Hugh was still 100 miles away from Fort Henry in North Dakota where he expected his old troop to be for the winter. The weather was brutal this time of year. You don't want to be walking in the North Dakota wilderness during the winter, but Hugh was determined. He was all alone again but was much healthier and better equipped than the last time he traveled solo. It took him over a month to get to the fort enduring freezing temperatures and horrible weather. He showed up on New Year's Eve, ready to bring doom with him for two unfortunate men.

At Fort Henry, Hugh found only one of the men, young Jim Bridger. Hugh didn't feel like someone that young should be held responsible. Jim was plenty terrified and apologetic when he saw Hugh. Apparently, Hugh's face was covered in the scars from the attack and he was extremely scary looking!

The other man, John Fitzgerald, had joined the army which meant Hugh would go to jail if he killed him. Hugh told him that the day he wasn't in the army anymore, he was a dead man. That must have made quite an impression on John. He stayed in the army until the day he died. Hugh lived out in the wilderness as a trapper for many more years. He never got his revenge, which was a good thing, but it sure motivated him through a difficult situation!

Keys to Survival: Hugh Glass was an extremely skilled survivalist. He had lived as a pirate, a Pawnee, a fur trapper mountain man...Hugh lived a truly adventurous life. The wounds he got from that bear attack should have killed him. That's what makes this such a spectacular story. He stayed close to water and had an intense determination to live. Scaring wolves away from their kill was very risky but it was smart to do it with fire. That saved his life. There's no doubt that Hugh was lucky as well. His wounds didn't get too badly infected and the native people that found him helped him. To survive something like that bear attack took a nearly superhuman will to live. Even though it came from his desire for revenge, which isn't a healthy way to think, it was enough to keep him alive.

Savior of the
"Saskatchewan Screamer"

This tale is as harrowing as it is inspiring. Lots of survival stories are also hero stories. Everyone is capable of being a hero. That's usually how it works. Heroism is usually demonstrated by someone who never thought of themselves as a hero. They just act when people need help. Sometimes kids are heroes. Sometimes they're 80 years old like Andre Bouvier Sr. More on him in a bit...

Saskatchewan is the Canadian province just north of North Dakota. It covers a lot of land (about the size of Texas) and winter temperatures can hit nearly 50 degrees below zero. So what's a Saskatchewan Screamer? Sounds scary, doesn't it? They sure can be. Saskatchewan is mostly prairie grassland, but to the north, it's rugged and rocky. This is where the arctic temperatures come from. When those cold weather fronts from the arctic come down and meet the warmer air from the Pacific that comes over the Rocky Mountains, you have the ingredients for a Saskatchewan Screamer.

This kind of storm is really quick moving, known for its extremely powerful winds and sideways flying snow. It can bring complete whiteout conditions and these screamers come up fast, catching people off guard. One minute you're out shopping and if you're not paying attention, you can find yourself in the middle of a howling blizzard. That's what happened to Shannon St. Onge as she was out running errands.

Shannon was the finance director of a University. On this day she had to drive 15 miles to the college to sign a check to help a student. The snow was starting to fall as she left the house, but Shannon thought she had time. Snow isn't unusual in Canada and the blizzard wasn't expected to hit for another four hours. She had a tank full of gas and grabbed a new charger for her phone. Those two things, along with the determination of an 80-year-old stranger would all add up to save her life that day.

She had been watching the weather and decided to take a dirt road as the highway roads might be too slippery with ice. She was right, but the problem was that it's easier to get lost driving on dirt roads. The ferocious unrelenting winds of the Saskatchewan Screamer had found Shannon. Much to the surprise of everyone, the storm was on its own schedule and came early. These winds were so fierce, that all of the snow that was on the ground was now flying everywhere making it impossible to see. Everything was white.

Shannon crept along with her window down so that she could see the side of the road. But soon, even that didn't work. She couldn't see anything. She had to stop. The wind did not stop. Shannon realized that she was in some serious trouble here. Where in the world was she and how would anyone possibly find her?

She called 911. The operator told her to stay calm and wait out the storm where she was. Driving was too dangerous. Since she had a full tank of gas, she could keep the heat on until the storm passed. Shannon sure hoped so! But how long would this storm last? She decided to get to work and find out where she was. She knew she couldn't walk far because she might not find the car again. The warm car was keeping her alive, but she was able to find a street sign in the swirling snow. It said, "Bouvier Lane."

Shannon used Google maps on her phone to pin her location and posted it on a local Facebook community page of her town along with a plea for help. People saw her post and started trying to help figure out where she was. She got a message from a guy who lived more than 1,000 miles away in Vancouver but was from her town. He knew Bouvier Lane and the family that lived there! He would call them and send help.

Andre Bouvier Sr. was home when he got the phone call about a woman stranded in her car not too far away. Andre was 80 years old but he wasn't the kind of guy to sit at home while someone was in trouble. His wife thought he was crazy and she was probably right. The storm was RAGING. He bundled up anyway and headed out. It was so cold that his tractor wouldn't start. Apparently, that didn't bother him too much. Andre grabbed a flashlight and began trudging into the storm on foot.

As long as he stayed on the road, he should be okay. But this was a Saskatchewan Screamer and Shannon's car was half a mile away. Andre would later say, "The worst part was the wind. Halfway there, I had to put my mitts in front of my eyes." But Andre stayed on the road and kept going.

He made it and it wasn't just Shannon's car there. He discovered two *more* cars of trapped people! Andre led them all back to his house one car at a time. He walked to where they were 3 times and back with each car following behind him as he walked. Andre and his wife welcomed a total of seven people out of the storm. Shannon said, "Once we arrived at the house, and I parked the car, I got out and jumped into his arms and gave him a great big bear hug. I was sobbing with gratitude, I was so grateful."

They all enjoyed a warm meal and laughed together as they ate. That had been a close one! That morning, the tractor started up and Andre was able to plow the driveway so that his new friends could drive home. The worst of the storm was over.

Shannon's Facebook post about her ordeal went viral and Andre was rightfully celebrated as a hero. But Andre, like most heroes, didn't want any credit. He said, "Everybody would have done the same thing. You don't think about it, you just do it."

Keys to Survival: Sometimes, even with our weather technology, storms can still surprise us. Shannon had smartly filled her car with gas and had a fully charged cell phone with a charger. Her car probably would have stayed on through the night keeping her warm. It was getting lost that put her in so much danger. If you don't know where you are, you can't tell people how to find you. She called 911 to let them know about her situation, and she didn't try to keep driving. It gets even harder to find someone if they accidentally drive off the road. Our hero, Andre, took a really big risk. Despite his age, he went out walking through a blizzard. Fortunately, he was somewhere he was very familiar with and could feel the road beneath his shoes. He made sure to stay on it. It was still very dangerous and that's what makes his act so heroic.

The Floor Really IS Lava!

You've probably seen the really fun and popular TV show, *The Floor Is Lava*. But it wasn't so fun for three men when their helicopter actually crashed into an active volcano! Yikes! How in the world did they make it out alive?

In sunny Hawaii there is an active volcano, called Kilauea. It has actually been active since 1983. That doesn't mean that it's always exploding and raining lava down on the heads of the people in Hawaii. It mostly just smolders. As I write this, it is technically in an eruption and there are lava flows into the ocean. But it's all a big tourist attraction. People aren't in any danger. You can still drive up to the top of the volcano and walk around.

So back to our story. How in the world does a helicopter crash into an active volcano? This happened in the early 1990s. A camera crew from the big movie studio, Paramount, was filming a scene for a movie. There weren't any actors there, they just needed footage of the volcano. As they were up above one of the active vents of the volcano, the helicopter suddenly began to lose control and fall from the sky. That's pretty terrible timing!

It all happened so fast that the pilot never had any time to radio a control tower and tell them to send help. There was no time for a mayday call as they were going down. The helicopter crashed inside the big volcano and was sitting there on the floor of the pit. They barely missed a big pool of lava that was bubbling and fizzing. It would be scary enough to be in a regular helicopter crash. I can't begin to imagine the terror of plummeting into a smoking volcano crater.

Luckily, they landed on dry ground down there. Even luckier, they were all alive and unharmed after the crash landing. The helicopter wasn't so lucky. It was lying there in two pieces. The men could have easily suffocated as soon as they crashed, but they managed to land in one part of Kilauea where there was oxygen. An active volcano tends to be filled with gasses like sulfur dioxide and hydrogen sulfide. Humans can't breathe in those gasses and stay alive. So these guys have been incredibly lucky so far despite crashing into a volcano which is rather unlucky.

The three men had no desire to hang out down there. They wanted to get out as fast as they could, so they started to climb. Climbing was difficult. The interior wall of the volcano would crumble as they moved on it. It was not dense so they constantly risked starting a rock slide. The pilot decided to go back to the helicopter and try to get the radio to work. That was a good move. He did get the radio working and a rescue helicopter came right away and was able to get down there and get him aboard. He didn't even have to wait very long.

But the two cameramen, Chris Duddy and Michael Benson were still halfway up the crater and weren't at all visible from the helicopter because of all of the volcanic gas. And because it was so loud in there, they had no idea that a rescue helicopter had flown in and gotten the pilot. They hadn't been able to see or hear it.

The crater of the volcano was 150 feet deep and Chris and Michael had managed to climb halfway up. That's where they spent a long and scary night. They could hear the lava down below them gurgling and crashing loudly like ocean surf. They didn't get any sleep. Neither of them thought they would survive.

The next day, Chris had enough and decided to try to climb the rest of the way out even though it seemed incredibly dangerous and difficult. Michael thought that was too risky. He had gotten to a little hole on the side of the crater that he wasn't in danger of falling from so he decided to stay there. They wished each other luck and Chris headed up.

That afternoon, Chris actually made it all the way up and out of the volcano which surprised even him. He had managed to climb a vertical wall of rock. It had taken him 27 hours to escape. He said the only reason he was brave enough to do that was thinking about his family.

Later that day, it rained a couple of times and Michael was able to get some water. He didn't have anything with him to help him survive. Sometimes he would hear eruptions from down below and thought he would die any minute. He understandably started to go a little crazy perched halfway up an active volcano crater. He started seeing things. He says he saw the legendary Hawaiian volcano goddess, Pele, on the other side of the volcano and he started yelling at her that she wasn't going to get him. He said "It was absolutely her. I wasn't hallucinating. It was just like being in the movies."

Michael spent two days with no food, no water, and no sleep. The reason he survived was that the steam around him stopped for the exact moment that a rescue helicopter pilot was looking in that direction. The pilot couldn't believe what he saw. He only caught a glimpse of Michael as the fog closed in right after he saw him. The trick now was to somehow get a rescue net close enough that Michael could grab it. The pilot only had a vague idea of where he was and would have to operate without being able to see him.

Michael didn't have much time left. His lungs and eyes were irritated, he was struggling to breathe, and he was completely dehydrated and a bit delirious as well. The rescue team above him could hear him and they yelled at him to look for a net. The helicopter pilot was flying blind, just guessing where Michael might be. The helicopter hovered right at the top of the crater and lowered the net. It landed right near Michael but got stuck on a rock. He managed to catch and hang on to the net on the second attempt.

As he was rising out of the volcano, he triumphantly yelled at the volcano goddess that he had won. All three men survived. They had even gotten the footage before the crash that they had set out to get. But after all that the men went through, their footage got cut from the movie. They weren't too happy about that, but they were sure happy to be out of that volcano!

Keys to Survival: In this case, staying at the crash site (even though it was scary and didn't feel safe) was the right decision. The pilot was rescued only hours after the crash. Even though Michael was in there the longest, he made the correct decision not to attempt climbing out. It would have been extremely easy to fall during that climb. Chris made a dangerous decision to attempt that climb without a rope. He felt panicked and couldn't stay in the volcano for another minute. It worked out for him, fortunately, but he was much younger than Michael and in better shape. All three men were extremely lucky. Active volcanoes are not something that you really want to see from the inside!

A Family in the Path of a Deadly Tsunami

It was their second trip to this beautiful land of white sandy beaches, palm trees, and ocean sunsets. The Squire family was back at the lovely Arugam Bay in the country of Sri Lanka. The weather and the water felt amazing. Little did they know that they were about to be in the middle of one of history's deadliest natural disasters.

A massive underwater earthquake along a deep-sea fault line in the Indian Ocean started it. There have only been two earthquakes that we know of that were bigger. That's how violent it was. It lasted nearly 10 minutes and caused the entire planet to tremble. The energy released by the earthquake was equal to 1,500 atomic bombs all exploding at once. For that to happen on the ocean floor, meant something really scary was about to happen at the surface. Huge killer waves, tsunamis, would soon spread out and head toward shore all around the Indian Ocean. These tsunamis would tragically end the lives of more than 227,000 people. The devastation was widespread and horrific.

Sri Lanka is an island country that is more than 1,000 miles away from where the earthquake happened. It's off the southern coast of India. The earthquake happened just before 8:00 in the morning. It took the tsunami around two hours to reach Sri Lanka. At the time (2004), there were no tsunami warning systems in the Indian Ocean. Tsunamis are rarer in that part of the world and much more common in the Pacific Ocean with its more active fault lines and earthquakes.

Emma Squire was in the hotel bathroom putting on her contact lenses. She was there with her mom, Louise, her dad, Phillip, her 19-year-old brother, Will, and her 21-year-old sister, Laura. Emma was 23. She heard her mom yell, "Emma!" just before water slammed into the room. The water went up to the ceiling and Emma couldn't breathe. What was happening? Then it went down pulling Emma out with it. She crashed into a palm tree and was lucky not to get knocked out. Water swirled all around her carrying cars, logs, and weird things like washing machines. It was very scary and extremely dangerous. This went on for 20 minutes before the water started to calm down and was no longer surging everywhere.

The next thing Emma sees is her father wading toward her. He had also landed in a palm tree. Amazingly, Emma and her dad came across both Laura and Will who were equally lucky. They frantically searched for Emma's mom but didn't see her anywhere.

The rest of her family didn't know, but Louise was okay! She had climbed a tree just like the others. She wasn't the only one with that idea as a snake was there, too, and bit her. Can this story get any scarier? After the snake bite, she was swarmed by ants who bit her. Louise eventually makes her way up a hill which was the highest point in the area and where many survivors were going. There was no sign of her family. Suddenly she heard her husband's voice as he and all three of her children ran to her and hugged her tight.

The family cried and cried as they embraced. All five of them had been separated and were beyond lucky to have all survived when so many others had not been so fortunate. The waves kept coming that day but although they were banged up, the Squire family was together and they were safe. To this day, there has never been a tsunami that has been as destructive as the one that the Squire family was so lucky to survive.

Keys to Survival: There was a lot of luck involved in this story. Emma talked about how dazed she was when she hit the palm tree and how easy it would be to just close her eyes and drift away. She says that she had to fight for her life clinging to that tree. In tsunami waters, it is very easy to die. There are lots of heavy things that can crush you or knock you unconscious, causing you to drown. Each family member was lucky to grab hold of something that didn't get swept away, like a tree. Some people at various places around the Indian Ocean noticed the water at the beach pulled far away from shore. That is a sure sign that a tsunami is on the way. Those that knew that, were able to run for safety. If you are somewhere close to the ocean and feel an earthquake, that is another warning sign that there might be dangerous waves headed your way. Find higher ground quickly or get as far from the beach as you can.

Surfer Kids to the Rescue!

More than 100 swimmers die every year because they get trapped in a rip current and drown. This is the story of two kids who got really lucky. Be sure to read the keys to survival section so this doesn't happen to you on your next beach vacation.

For the four surfer buddies, it was just another day at the beach. Taj Ortiz-Beck was 15 years old. His three friends were just 16. They were Adrian York, Narayan Weibel, and Spenser Stratton. They all lived in Northern California and loved surfing. Trinidad State Beach offered the friends a great place to do it.

It was early November and the boys had been surfing for a couple of hours. The water was cold that time of year so they were all wearing wetsuits. The water was just over 50 degrees which is quite chilly. Taj, Adrian, Narayan, and Spenser often went surfing when they got done with soccer practice. Narayan and Spenser had attended the local lifeguard program that summer.

The four friends were all taking a break floating on their boards when it happened. It was Veterans Day, a holiday weekend, so there were more people out enjoying the beach than usual. Two brothers had been out there swimming around in the cold water. They weren't dressed for it at all. They were 20 and 15 years old. They hadn't planned on being out long. That's when they both found themselves in big trouble. A rip current had them.

Rip currents can form anywhere there are breaking waves. The more powerful the waves, the more powerful the rip current can be. They can be hard to spot which means they catch many swimmers off guard. They are narrow, fast-moving currents moving back out to sea. Being narrow, they are easy to get out of but many people panic and try to swim straight back to shore. That's just not possible.

That's what happened to the two brothers at Trinidad State Beach. Their family lost sight of them quickly because it was foggy that day. They could only hear their screams. That must have been terrifying for everyone. Not only is it hard to swim against a rip current, but it's really hard to swim in cold water. The two brothers were already exhausted. They were having a hard time getting air above the water.

The four surfer friends heard the screams and saw the flailing arms. Narayan said that the four boys all looked at each other and knew that it was up to them to save the drowning swimmers. Adrian quickly paddled to shore to get someone to call 911 before heading back out to help.

Taj was the first to get to the younger of the two brothers in trouble. He says, "It was pretty stressful, but there wasn't any time to think about it, and that helped me keep my cool." Taj pulled the boy up onto his board. That left Spenser and Narayan to pull in the 20-year-old brother. He was much larger and was completely panicked. Narayan yelled, "Calm down! We got you!" Adrian got there just in time to help pull the guy up onto one of the boards. Later, Narayan explained, "Being out in that cold water without a wet suit is like taking an ice bath. They were having a hard time keeping their heads above water and thought they were going to die."

The boys paddled back to shore to the panicked family members as fast as they could. They made sure the two brothers were still breathing and it didn't take medics long to get to the beach. There was no doubt that the four friends had just saved two lives by taking fast action and getting to the swimmers so quickly. They were proud heroes.

Keys to Survival: Eight out of ten beach lifeguard rescues are saving people from rip currents. When getting pulled away from the beach by one of these sneaky currents, most people panic. That's the worst thing you can do in any survival situation, and a rip current is most definitely that. One minute you're enjoying a beach swim, and the next minute you're fighting for your life. The good thing is that it's really easy to escape a rip current. You just have to swim parallel with the beach and because rip currents are narrow, you won't have to swim far to escape it. What you can't do is swim directly back to the beach from inside the rip current. You will get tired and then not be able to keep your head above the water. The key is to realize what is happening, and then remember these words...*swim parallel to the beach*. You will soon be out of the current and only then can you swim back to the safety of the shore. If you see this happening to someone, try to throw them something that floats (like a life preserver) and let rescuers know right away.

A Mountain Miracle

Mountaineering is a really dangerous pastime, but some people love it. There are lots of ways that things can go wrong climbing up the world's tallest mountains. It's very cold up there. It's icy and easy to fall. But Joe Simpson and Simon Yates had worked together before, and there they were, standing on the very top of Siula Grande in the Andes Mountains in Peru. They had done it! They were the first people to ever climb up the dangerous West Face of the mountain. Their names would go down in mountaineering history. Little did they know that they would be much more famous for what they were about to survive.

Descending back down the mountain that a climber has just climbed, is often the most dangerous part of the journey. That's when the climbers are really tired from having already climbed up the mountain. 85% of all mountaineering accidents happen on the way back down. Joe was climbing down an ice cliff. He swung one of his ice axes into the ice and the ice just fell away which made Joe fall. He landed at the bottom of the cliff and was in a lot of pain. He had broken his right ankle and heel. His knee was crushed with torn ligaments. He could no longer walk and that's a huge problem when you're climbing down a 6,000-foot mountain that's covered in snow and ice.

When Simon got down to him and saw that Joe's leg was broken, he was devastated. Getting down would be really hard for two *healthy* climbers. Now, one of them was completely helpless. Simon would have to lower Joe down the mountain. Simon would lower Joe for as far as his rope would let him and then Joe would get his weight off of the rope while Simon climbed down to where he was. They got Joe down 300 feet and would have to do that 10 more times. It was exhausting work for Simon but so far so good.

They were going down the other side of the mountain from where they had climbed as they thought it would be safer. So Joe slid off the edge of the cliff and found himself dangling 150 feet in the air with no way to climb back up the rope. Both of his hands were frostbitten. This meant that they were so cold that he could no longer use them. Simon had no way to pull him back up. They couldn't even talk or yell to each other. The wind was too loud.

Nightfall was coming. It would be dark soon. Simon held on for hours. But he knew that eventually he would fall and they would both die. He made the agonizing decision to cut the rope sending Joe falling to his death. Joe had been hanging there in the freezing wind for what seemed like days. And then without warning...he was falling.

He plummeted 150 feet and fell through the ice into a crevasse. A crevasse is a crack in the ice. They can be 500 feet deep with no way out. As scary as that sounds, if Joe had landed just a few feet away, he would have fallen another 3,000 feet down the mountain. He was also lucky not to have broken any more bones in the fall. He was on a small ledge 70 feet down inside the ice crevasse. There was no way to climb out. Below him was only darkness. When he landed, he thought that Simon must have fallen too. But when he pulled on the rope, it all fell down and he saw that it had been cut. Joe wasn't mad, he was happy that Simon was still alive.

Simon was exhausted and depressed about his friend. He needed rest. He dug a snow cave to wait out the night. He would climb down tomorrow. Meanwhile, Joe was thinking about what to do. He did the only thing he could do. He climbed further down in the crevasse hoping that his luck would continue. There was a slope that he could slide down. And eventually, there was a slope back up. He crawled and crawled and finally saw sunlight! He popped his head out of the crevasse and laughed and laughed.

He saw Simon's rope where he had climbed down and passed on his way. This meant that Simon had already passed by and his survival was now completely up to him. Simon had found the crevasse on his way down and called down to Joe not knowing that Joe was crawling up in another part of it. He assumed that Joe was dead when he didn't hear anything and that's perfectly reasonable. Joe realized that he was still 8 miles away from base camp. That meant that he would somehow have to crawl another 8 miles in order to get out of this alive. It seemed more like 800 miles!

Joe was dehydrated and hadn't had any water to drink. He was also suffering from the cold and frostbite. It had been more than 24 hours since he had broken his leg, but he started to crawl. He had to be careful not to fall down another ice crevasse. He kept this up for 3 more days. He would just focus on small goals. Crawl to that rock in 30 minutes and he would be happy if he did it. Then he would make another goal and keep going. After 3 days of this, he was in really bad shape. He was starving and going crazy. He kept passing out and seeing things that weren't there.

He eventually made it to within a 10-minute walk of base camp where he thought he might find help. But crawling in the state that he was in, took him another 9 hours. It had now been 4 days since he had fallen down into the crevasse. As Joe got closer to base camp, he realized that Simon probably wasn't there anymore. That would mean that he would die for sure. Simon was actually still there but about to leave. Simon had needed recovery time after his climb down so he had spent the last few days resting and thinking about how he was going to tell people that he had cut the rope, killing his climbing partner.

Just before Simon was about to leave, he saw Joe. He couldn't believe it! Joe could hardly believe it either. He was barely alive and still had to survive riding a mule for 2 days just to get to their truck. It would take another entire day to get to a hospital. Joe's ordeal lasted for 11 days, but he was finally safe in a hospital bed. He had made it.

Keys to Survival: The perseverance that Joe Simpson had to find in order to survive is amazing to me. It was incredible determination. He ate snow to stay hydrated which you have to do if you don't have water. This is necessary, but dangerous because it lowers your body's temperature which is especially threatening in the cold. One of the key things here is how he broke up the 8 miles he had to crawl. It's an overwhelming distance and it would be easy to give up if he kept thinking about it as 8 miles. But he broke it up into 20-foot chunks and that's all he focused on. Keep going 20 feet at a time. That's a really effective way to avoid giving up.

Man Survives 18 Days
Trapped in Attic

You have probably heard about Hurricane Katrina. It was a devastating hurricane to hit New Orleans, Louisiana in 2005. Nearly 2,000 people died. It was a terrible tragedy. Out of this, came many stories of heroism and survival. This hurricane was so deadly because of the flooding that came with it. New Orleans is a city that sits below sea level. It had levees that were designed to prevent the city from flooding, but they were breached by the massive storm. Eighty percent of the city was underwater.

These floods cut off tens of thousands of people from help and supplies. One of those people was 76-year-old Gerald Martin. Everyone knew that a bad storm was coming, but few realized how destructive it would be. Gerald's family had left, but he didn't want to miss church, so he stayed. He laid down to take a nap and wait for the storm to come. He woke up to find his house filling up with water!

Fortunately, he moved quickly. He grabbed as much drinking water as he could and went up into his attic. It was August, so it was hot in New Orleans. Have you ever been in an attic on a hot day in the Summer? It can be unbearable. After the storm passed, the temperature got up into the 90s. That meant that it could have been around 125-130 degrees in Gerald's attic. That can not only be uncomfortable, it can be deadly. One thing that may have saved Gerald from dealing with that amount of heat was a tree that fell on his roof. It didn't cave in the roof, but it did keep the roof shaded from the sun. So while it was still really hot in that attic, the temperature didn't rise to dangerous levels.

Gerald was wishing that he had grabbed some food too, but he didn't expect to be stranded for that long. As the days turned into weeks, he rationed the amount of water that he drank, but he was running out. That's a really long time to go without eating. He had lost a lot of weight. The attic feeling like an oven didn't help much.

Eighteen days after the hurricane had hit, rescuers weren't finding many survivors, but they were still searching each house. A boat pulled up to 6010 Painters St. As they did, they heard a voice! "Hey, over here." They grabbed a sledgehammer and broke through the front door. The house was gross. Water had been up to the ceiling for 16 days and had just gone down. The house was still surrounded by water but at least it was no longer full of it. This had allowed Gerald to finally come down out of the attic after 16 days up there. Rescuers found him sitting in his kitchen. Everything was covered in sludge.

Gerald was dehydrated and starving. He had run out of water and may not have survived another day without it. He was loaded up on a helicopter and really happy. He wasn't even mad when the helicopter driver didn't take him to a Taco Bell like he asked. He would get a burrito soon enough. He had made it.

Keys to Survival: When Gerald realized that he was in trouble, he made some good, quick decisions. He grabbed water. It was only a gallon and a half but that is what kept him alive. 18 days is a long time to be by yourself. It would have been easy to panic or to give up, but Gerald did neither. He rationed his water, and stayed patient. Eventually, rescuers got to him.

Teenager Falls 10,000 Feet & Lands in the Jungle

It was Christmas Eve. 17-year-old Juliane and her mom were going on a one-hour flight to see Juliane's dad. They were flying from Lima, Peru to the town of Pucallpa. Her dad was an ecologist there. Juliane had grown up in Peru with both of her parents working for a museum and conducting research. Juliane's mom was a scientist as well, who was an expert on birds.

Juliane's mom was nervous about the flight. It was stormy. The pair sat in the back of the plane and away they went. There were 91 people on the plane. After being in the air for 25 minutes, disaster struck. Juliane saw lightning strike the wing. The plane started to fall. As it was going down, it began to fall apart and Juliane's seat was ripped away and out of the plane. Can you imagine? (This happened more than 50 years ago, air travel is much safer these days.)

As she was falling two miles down to earth, Juliane thought the trees looked like broccoli. She passed out. The good news is that she woke up! The bad news is that she was alone in the Amazon rainforest and was really hurt. Her collarbone was broken. That's the bone that connects your shoulder to your sternum (the bone in the middle of your chest) and it's a really painful injury.

One of her eyes was swollen shut and the other was almost swollen shut but she could see out of it a little. She wore glasses but they were long gone. She had also lost her sandals, but other than some cuts, sprains, and her broken collarbone, she was okay. Her plane seat had landed on some big soft plants that helped absorb the impact of her fall. It was a miracle for her to be alive. Still, she was alone and scared. She sat there crying for a while in the rain and she was soaking wet and really muddy. It was the Amazon's rainy season. This meant that there wasn't any fruit around for Juliane to eat. All she had for food was a bag of candy.

Growing up near the jungle, her parents had told her how to survive if she ever got lost. The main goal was to find water and follow it. Streams turn into rivers, and people live near rivers. After some wandering around that first day, she did it. She found a stream. Now she knew where to go. She had to watch out for alligators though. There were also poisonous spiders, snakes, and stingrays. There were bees that would fly all around her face, fortunately not the stinging kind but still pretty terrible. And there were, of course, mosquitos. There were lots and lots of mosquitos.

On and on, Juliane went. She walked and walked. She ran out of candy. She drank water from the stream and then from the river that it ran into. She continued downstream. She kept this up for 11 days. That's some serious determination! Starving, wounded, and dealing with all the bugs and the heat, all without shoes or being able to see well, this was a nightmare. The cuts on her leg and arms from the fall were not doing well and had become infected. Juliane was in rough shape when she finally stumbled across a hut.

It belonged to loggers. And fortunately, they were nearby! They fed her and treated her wounds. They took her to a village where people were able to get her more help and get her to a hospital. Juliane was the only survivor of that plane crash. She was reunited with her father and became a scientist herself. Now she is in charge of the biological research facility that her father worked at, carrying on her parents' legacy. She continues to make scientific discoveries related to the wildlife that lives in the Amazon.

Keys to Survival: For Juliane to keep up her search for civilization for 11 days in the condition she was in, is remarkable. It's also incredible that she survived that fall from the plane. What saved her (other than her tenacity and willpower) was following water. Following water will usually always lead you to people who will help you. The water will also keep you alive as you go. You can survive for weeks without food, but only a few days without water.

The Original Mountain Man,
The Legend of John Colter

I'm going to introduce you to one heck of a character from American history, John Colter. John was a frontiersman in the early 1800s. His adventures are legendary. Living in Kentucky, John saw an advertisement that was searching for, "good hunters, stout, healthy, unmarried men, accustomed to the woods, and capable of bearing bodily fatigue in a pretty considerable degree."

Those words were written by Meriwether Lewis to William Clark. Have you heard of Lewis and Clark? They were the guys that, along with Sacagawea, went on the great exploration of the American West for Thomas Jefferson. Meriwether had asked William to find these able-bodied adventurers to go along on this historic journey. John signed up and joined them.

They would pay John $5 per month. He stayed with them for quite some time on their expedition. They went all the way to the Pacific Ocean and back. John was a key member of the expedition and both Lewis and Clark relied on him heavily. He was well known for both his hunting skills and his ability to trade with native people. John was so crucial to the success of the expedition, that he earned the praise and gratitude of President Thomas Jefferson. On the way back, John got Lewis and Clark's permission to leave with some fur trappers. The expedition was nearly over and John thought it would be a good opportunity for money and adventure. They headed north for Yellowstone.

A couple of years later, John was put on another mission. This time, to build a fort in what is now Yellowstone National Park. It would be called Fort Raymond. John was sent ahead to set up trade with the Blackfeet Native Americans who were prevalent in that area. Along the way, he made friends with a party of Crow Native Americans. The Crow were enemies of the Blackfeet. When the Crow tribe that John was traveling with was attacked by Blackfeet warriors, he joined in the fight. Now John was an enemy of the Blackfeet, too.

After recovering from his wounds, he set out on another trade mission. This time he was with another frontiersman, John Potts, who he had traveled with on the Lewis and Clark expedition. The two Johns were in the Yellowstone wilderness camping along the Yellowstone river when John Colter, once again, found himself being attacked by the Blackfeet. He told John Potts that their only hope was surrender. But Potts shot and killed one of the Blackfeet after being struck by an arrow. The warriors killed him quickly and moved in.

Now John Colter was all by himself and surrounded by Blackfeet warriors who were deciding what to do with him. The Blackfeet didn't know it but John could understand their language a little. One of the warriors wanted to tie him to a tree and use him for target practice. Yikes. But the guy in charge had another idea. He had the men take John's clothes. The elder warrior told John that he would be hunted. The Blackfeet would give him a head start. Then he said..."RUN."

John didn't wait around. He sprinted off. He could hear the warriors yell out their war cries as they chased him. Fortunately, John was fast and also good at running quickly through the forest. He decided that he would have to hide somewhere really sneaky in order to survive. So he ran back the way he had come toward the river where he was first attacked. The river might provide the best hiding spots.

One of the warriors was faster than the rest and chased John down. John could hear him getting close and spun around to face him. This startled his attacker who was armed with a spear. Because he was startled, the warrior tripped as he threw the spear. This gave John the chance he needed. John raced off, made it to the water, and jumped in. He had run about 5 miles.

In the water, he swam under an old beaver dam. That was some luck finding that! This allowed him to breathe but stay completely hidden from view. The warriors didn't find him despite searching all night for him. He shivered in his hiding spot until he was sure that the war party had moved on. His feet were badly hurt from running barefoot through the woods as fast as he could during the hunt. He didn't have anything at all, not even clothes! John was naked in the woods, in hostile territory, miles from a town or any help.

John was an extremely experienced frontiersman by this point. He ate plants and weeds as he walked for 11 days to a fort that he was familiar with. Luckily, it wasn't winter! Even so, I sure wouldn't want to be in that situation. He lost a lot of weight, but he survived. As he told his story in front of a warm fire at the fort, the legend of "Colter's Run" was born.

John spent several years after that exploring the mountain ranges to the north. He stayed mostly by himself leaving many to call him the first true American mountain man. He eventually left the mountains and got married in Missouri. He met up again with William Clark who John helped create the most comprehensive map of the American West. John was the only man alive to have explored many of the places so his information was invaluable. His legacy as the original American mountain man lives on to this day.

A Mind-Boggling WWII
Arctic Survival Story

All hope was lost. The top secret mission had failed. They had been discovered by the Nazis. The Norwegian commando climbed out of the frigid waters of Toftefjord Bay with his uniform completely frozen. He heard gunfire behind him. He had no time. They were coming for him. He ran down a small hill and hid behind a rock. He was shivering terribly. His friends were already dead or captured and he could see four German soldiers coming for him. Covered in ice, he pulled out his gun with frozen fingers and waited.

It was 1943 and World War II was raging. Norway was controlled by the Germans. And that was important because Norway was the gateway to the North Sea which encircled England. The British, in order to win this war, knew that they would have to win the North Sea. Hitler knew that too, so he moved his German forces into Norway in order to tighten his grip around England.

In Norway, a secret resistance army was formed to fight back against the Nazis. One unit was the Norwegian Independent Company 1. Their job was to sabotage German military boats and planes and to weaken the German forces in any way that they could. At the end of March 1943, four of the company's commandos along with eight men as a boat crew, set out on a secret mission. This mission was to sneak into a German air base and blow up their planes.

This air base was way up in the northern part of Norway, 200 miles inside the Arctic Circle.

They attempted to set up contact with someone friendly to their cause, but that person notified the Germans. When they found out that their mission was compromised, they tried to escape on their boat which was full of the explosives to be used on their mission. They set out into the fjords to escape but were cut off by a German war boat. They didn't want their bombs to be used by the Nazis so they deployed a life raft and blew up their boat, the Brattholm. That's when the Germans opened fire on them and sank the raft, killing some of the men.

Most of the men were pulled out of the water by the Germans as prisoners. Some were dead. But one of them managed to swim over to a small island. That man was Jan Baalsrud. This is the incredible story of how he managed to escape 125 miles through the Arctic Circle, all while being hunted by the German army.

Jan pulled the trigger. Nothing happened. His gun was frozen and he was running out of time. The four German soldiers were getting closer. He took the magazine out and got rid of the first two bullets. This time the gun worked. He shot two of the soldiers and the other two retreated. One of Jan's boots was gone and everything was covered in snow. His uniform had turned into a sheet of ice. Jan knew that being captured meant certain death, so off he went.

He went back into the Arctic water to get off the island on the other side, away from the Germans. Night fell as he went. Luckily, Jan ran into two girls who walked him back to their house. The family decided to help him even though it was extremely risky for them. The Germans were close and if they discovered the family helping an enemy, they might all be killed. They got Jan dried off and warmed up. They fed him and let him rest. As he left, he told the girls not to tell anyone that they had seen him. They would all die if the Germans found out.

Jan knew that he was endangering anyone who helped him. So he always kept his helpers' names a secret, even from others who helped him. There was no way to tell who was for or against the Nazis. If he asked the wrong person for help, he could be killed. Northern Norway is very mountainous. Even though it was April now, in this part of the world it was still winter. The going was tough. When Jan was starving and freezing, he would knock on doors. Somehow, he was always lucky. People helped him, but he had to keep moving.

Villagers would give him new boots, food, and warm places to sleep. His feet were horribly frostbitten from the cold, and the people he met would help him with bandages as well. Most people did not like that the Germans had taken over their country and were willing to help a fellow Norwegian who was a fugitive resistance fighter. He was even given a pair of skis to help him go faster. He once quickly skied past a small group of German soldiers before they could check him out. On his skis, he was caught in a blizzard. He couldn't see a thing and as he was working his way over a mountain, he was blasted by an avalanche!

He was buried neck deep in the snow but managed to crawl out although his skis were destroyed and his bag of supplies was lost. He was delirious and struggling badly and the blizzard would not let up. He suffered from snow blindness and wandered around for 3 days in the storm. Finally, he was lucky enough to wander into a village where a family hid him in their barn. A house nearby happened to be full of German soldiers. Jan was lucky not to stagger into that house! It was here that his frostbitten feet had gotten so bad during his blizzard ordeal that he couldn't walk any further. Still being hunted by the Germans made his dangerous situation even worse. Two German soldiers actually performed a routine search of the barn that he was hiding in but failed to check the loft. The family found others sympathetic to the cause, and a wooden stretcher was made. They put him on a sled and got him to a rowboat which took him across another fjord.

There, they put Jan in a small wooden shed with supplies where he could reach them. Jan had a sense of humor and called the shed, "Hotel Savoy", which was a famous, fancy hotel in London. There was no heat in this shed and the temperatures would get down well below freezing at night. Another snowstorm came which left him stranded there for another five days all alone. During this time, he did something important but really gross in order to survive. He had to cut off several of his toes to prevent gangrene from spreading on his feet. I know that's gross! This was an extreme survival situation and poor Jan did what he had to do.

Sympathizers finally came and moved him along for many miles. They left him up a mountain where he stayed for another 9 days in a snow cave they dug out for him. Then he was moved to an open mountain top where he spent 5 days and nearly went crazy. When people came for him there, Jan was in such bad shape that he asked them to just let him die. Instead, they kept moving him closer to Sweden and left him in a cave where he would survive another 17 days. Here, in order to save his feet, he cut off the rest of his toes as they were so damaged by frostbite. Eventually, some native tribal people called the Sami, took Jan on a sled pulled by reindeer through Finland to the Swedish border. The Germans were on his trail the entire time. They wanted him badly. By this point, Jan weighed 80 pounds. He had been near death for a month now, but still, he hung on.

He finally made it to a hospital in Sweden, a full two months after being attacked by German troops. He would spend another six months there recovering. He had to learn how to walk again. That's hard when you don't have any toes! But Jan, even after all he had gone through, couldn't stand by while others were in danger. He couldn't abandon the resistance effort. After he had recovered, he went to Scotland to help train resistance fighters. Later, he even went back to Norway (still controlled by the Germans) to keep fighting. While he was there, the war ended and Norway was a free country once again.

Jan Baalsrud became a national symbol and a Norwegian folk hero. His story of survival might be the most improbable and difficult in this entire book. It's a testament to both his astounding determination and the inspiring courage of regular people all across Norway who risked their lives to save him.

10-Year-Old Lost
in the Utah Mountains

Ten year old Malachi Bradley loved camping with his family, and that's what they were going to do. It was the end of August and they had backpacked to Paul Lake in Utah and set up their camp. It is a beautiful spot in the Ashley National Forest in the northern part of the state. It's over 10,000 feet in elevation. It's very mountainous.

The family had settled in to enjoy a beautiful day. Malachi was fishing for his lunch and he caught one! It was a good-sized trout. He had been reading about wild mushrooms and wanted to find some to cook with his fish. So he went hiking to pick some. It was 10:30 in the morning. Malachi's family wouldn't see him until 30 hours later.

His parents noticed that he was missing pretty quickly. They called for him and looked all around. Malachi had vanished. Even though it hadn't been long, they were extremely nervous. Malachi's dad had an uneasy feeling so he hiked back to the car and drove until he got a phone signal. He reported Malachi missing and asked for help. He got it. A rescue search was put together quickly. Helicopters were launched to find the missing boy, but nobody could find him anywhere.

Malachi had walked farther than he realized and got turned around which is easy to do in the Utah backcountry. When he realized that he was lost, he decided to stay put. His family camped and hiked a lot. He had gotten a little bit of survival training from his dad. Fortunately, Malachi had his coat with him. He would need it. What he didn't have was food or water. Instead of drinking muddy water, he turned his hoodie inside out and used it as a water filter to get water from puddles. That was pretty smart.

As the sun went down with no sign of his parents, it started to get cold. Malachi climbed up a hill behind some big rocks to protect himself from the wind. The temperature got down into the 30s. That's cold! And because the wind would shift and come from different directions, Malachi had to keep moving his body behind different rocks throughout the night. He didn't sleep well, but he made it.

The next day, he went out into an open area so that he could best be seen by helicopters. A couple flew over him without seeing him but at 3:00 that afternoon, he was finally noticed by one. Malachi was happy not to have to hike back. He was rescued 5 miles from where he had left his family.

Malachi was very brave throughout his ordeal and remained calm. It's really important if you're hiking by yourself (even just a little ways), that you don't lose track of where you've come from. It's easier to get lost than you might think!

Keys to Survival: Fortunately, Malachi didn't have to wait too long to get rescued. The most important thing for him was to not get too cold and to find water to drink. You can't go too long without water. Malachi kept a really cool head and was able to get water from some puddles by sucking it through his sweatshirt to avoid drinking mud. That was a great trick! It was also helpful that he didn't keep walking. That usually makes it harder for rescuers to find you.

Left for Dead on Mount Everest

He suddenly hopped up as the blizzard raged and yelled, "I've got this all figured out!" And with those words, he was knocked down and disappeared into the darkness.

Beck Weathers was a Texan who worked studying diseases as a pathologist. He became fascinated with the act of mountaineering, or climbing tall mountains. He got really into it. Eventually, he found himself attempting to climb to the top of the tallest mountain on earth, Mount Everest.

Unfortunately for Beck, he had eye surgery before his trip. As he kept getting higher and higher up the mountain, his vision kept getting worse. Although a blind person has made it to the top of Everest before, it's really helpful to be able to see when you're climbing mountains. Especially if everyone on your team isn't expecting you to become blind up there. One wrong step can mean death on Everest.

Rob Hall was a professional mountaineer. He was getting paid to take eight clients up the mountain and Beck was one of them. When you climb Everest, you do some of your climbing at night. As night fell, Beck's vision got even worse. He knew that he wouldn't be able to make it to the top. Rob told him that the safest thing to do was to wait where he was and the rest of the group would help him down after they had been to the top. They would meet back up with Beck on their way down.

Beck was pretty grumpy about this but realized that he had no choice. His dream of getting to the top of the world's tallest mountain would have to wait. While Beck waited there, other teams were passing him on their way back down. Several offered to take him down with them. The weather was getting worse. Beck told them that he was waiting on his team and Rob. This would turn out to be a really bad decision. He would never see Rob again.

The team that Beck had been climbing with made it to the summit of Everest and celebrated. Unfortunately, tragedy was right around the corner. As they made their way down from the top, one of the team members started to struggle. Rob sent everyone else down and stayed behind with him.

Word got to Beck that Rob was stuck with a struggling client further up the mountain. Beck still wanted to wait for one of the team members, Mike Groom. Eventually, Mike got to Beck, and Beck was finally headed down the mountain. There was a camp that they were hoping to rest at, but a blizzard hit before they got there.

It's hard to do much of anything in a blizzard. Climbing down Mount Everest is really hard on a good day. Mike was leading Beck and eight other climbers. They got lost in the blizzard. The snow made it nearly impossible for any of them to see anything. The trail they were supposed to be on had disappeared.

After sitting there being blasted by the blizzard for a few hours, the storm let up. But Beck and several others were too weak to continue. So Beck and three other climbers stayed where they were. The other climbers went down to the camp to get help. Help would come, but too late for Beck. When the rescuers got to where the four climbers were, there were only three. Beck was gone.

Beck had somehow lost a glove which was a dangerous mistake. If any of your skin is exposed to the air, you risk getting frostbite. It's simply too cold up there. When you add a blizzard to the mix, it becomes especially dangerous. Beck's mental state was coming unglued. He doesn't remember what he was thinking, but to the other climbers' surprise, he jumped up and yelled, "I've got this all figured out!" They were the words of a man who had become delirious and didn't know what he was doing. As soon as he got the words out, the wind blew him off the ledge and down the mountain.

The other climbers figured he was dead, and that was a reasonable assumption. But Beck eventually came to his senses. Unfortunately, he was in a terrible predicament. He didn't know where he was. He had spent the night exposed to the cold, laying there by himself.

Somehow he found the will to stand up and start moving. He still wasn't able to see very well, but he had just enough eyesight and determination to pull off a miracle. Climbers couldn't believe it when they saw him stagger into the camp that he had been trying to get to the day before. That was the good news. The bad news was he was in rough shape. His face was nearly completely black with frostbite. So were his hands.

People thought that all they could do for him was to help him get as comfortable as possible before he died. But after another night in a tent, he was somehow still alive! That was a big surprise to everyone. Without the use of his hands, he couldn't drink anything or keep the sleeping bags on top of him. And yet, he was still alive the next morning.

Beck's feet were frozen at this point so it was difficult to get him down to the next camp. He managed to get there. Nobody thought Beck would be alive much longer if they didn't get him off the mountain as soon as possible. His rescue was the highest that a rescue helicopter had ever gone to get a climber off of a mountain.

Beck luckily survived an extremely painful nightmare. Because the frostbite damage was so bad, he lost his nose, fingers from his left hand, his right arm, and some toes. Yikes! Doctors were able to make a brand-new nose for him. Incredibly, Beck says that he was glad that it all happened! He was so grateful to be alive that he was much nicer to everyone after he recovered. His relationship with his wife and family got much better.

He had this to say about his ordeal, "I gave up some body parts, but I got back my marriage, I got back my relationship with my kids, I've got a new grandbaby...all in all, if I had to do it again, every pain, every misery, every bit of suffering that comes from it, I'd do it again in a heartbeat."

Keys to Survival: Most mountain climbers on Everest who end up in Beck's condition don't survive. He was lucky, but he also had an incredible will to live. He had been left for dead and through sheer determination, hiked down to camp. That saved his life. He could have made better decisions on the mountain, but he didn't know that a blizzard was about to hit. He waited because he was hoping that his eyesight would improve when the sun came back up. He would have avoided a lot of suffering if he had gone down earlier when he had the chance. It sounds like he wouldn't change anything about his experience which is a great attitude to have. We can't change the past. We have to live with it, and Beck is doing that.

Mudslide!

She looked up and there was a huge tree standing in the middle of the highway. What in the world? It was moving! The couple watched in horror through the windshield of their car as the tree was quickly pushed over the cliff by a great river of mud. Suddenly the mud had them too, and they hurtled down the 4,000-foot cliff. They didn't even have time to hit the brakes.

This was supposed to be such a fun trip! Sheri Niemegeers and Gabe Rosescu had been dating for half a year and really liked each other. They had planned a 760-mile road trip to go see some friends in the British Columbia province of Canada from Sheri's home in Saskatchewan. They would drive through the majestic Canadian Rocky Mountains.

The Canadian Rockies are glorious and beautiful. They're more jagged and everything is bigger compared to the American Rockies. Lots of people love making that trip and driving on the scenic highway through the mountains. It was the month of May and unknown to Sheri and Gabe, there had been a lot of flooding going on due to heavy rain. This can create a dangerous situation when there are steep mountain ranges.

This was also the time of year when snow melts. That can cause a mudslide, too. The ground becomes loose, turns into mud, and begins to slide. The mud starts picking up everything in its path as it gets stronger and

stronger. Sheri and Gabe were extremely unlucky to be driving along in the path of such a strong mudflow. They were also unlucky to be next to a steep cliff.

It definitely could have been worse. They had some good luck, too. Instead of falling the full 4,000 feet to their death, their car miraculously came to rest on a cliff ledge 900 feet down from the highway that they had been on. This would be incredibly difficult to escape from, but at least they were alive. Sheri and Gabe were both knocked unconscious. When Sheri woke up, she was in a lot of pain, but she was in better shape than poor Gabe. He was still unconscious and moaning. Several bones in his face and parts of his skull were broken.

Sheri's left ankle was completely crushed with her foot sticking out at a weird angle. She tried to open the car door. That's when she felt it. She had terrible chest pain. She didn't know it at the time, but she had a broken sternum. That's the bone that goes right down the middle of your chest and all of your ribs connect to it. It also protects your heart.

These two were not going to be able to climb the 900 feet up the steep slope through all of the mud. But they weren't going down either. That way was a 3,000-foot drop to the river at the bottom of the gorge. It's hard to imagine a more dangerous situation. The car had barely held together. The two doors were crushed and surrounded by mud. There was no getting out that way. There were trees that had been swept up in the mudslide that were blocking Sheri's window.

Neither Sheri nor Gabe remember climbing out of the car, but they had to have gone through Gabe's window as it was the only way out. They sat down on a fallen tree and thought about what to do. Their phones didn't have a signal to call for help. What would you do? Sheri and Gabe did the only thing they could think of and it was a long shot. There didn't seem to be any other options at all. Despite the hopelessness of their situation, they yelled for help from their little cliff ledge 900 feet down from the road.

Amazingly, someone yelled back! Four men happened to hear them and were rushing down the hill to help. Two of them were firefighters who weren't working that day. Those two were Dan Anderson and Marty Bowes. They had been up on the highway filming the destruction with their phones when they heard Sheri and Gabe's calls for help. It took them a while to get there because of how steep the hill was and all the mud they had to wade through but they eventually got there. Two of the men started helping Gabe up and out. Gabe was a mess but he could walk. Sheri couldn't walk with her broken ankle. She would have to be carried.

So the other two guys picked up Sheri and started to climb. Eventually, one would get completely stuck in the waist deep mud and they would stop. The two men helping Gabe would pick up Sheri while the other guy who wasn't stuck would help the stuck rescuer out of the mud. The four rescuers would go back and forth like this for an hour. Carrying someone up a steep muddy slope was no picnic. The mud was really deep in places.

By the time they got back to the road, Gabe was passing out every few minutes and was in shock. They didn't have to wait long for medics to arrive and it's a good thing. Sheri was whisked away to a hospital not far away and Gabe was taken to a waiting helicopter where he was flown to a special hospital because his injuries were so severe. The medics had to continually shock him during the 260-mile flight so he didn't fall into a coma that he might not have woken up from.

It took 6 weeks and several surgeries to put Gabe's skull back together again. He lost vision in one of his eyes. Sheri will always have a limp because of her crushed ankle, but they lived through their ordeal and stuck together. They even still go on lots of road trips and bravely went back to the scene of their near-death experience on Canada's Crowsnest Highway. Their experience made them extremely grateful for every day of their lives. They no longer worry as much or get as annoyed by minor things. They should be dead, but they're not, and they now live with a powerful appreciation for each breath that they take.

Keys to Survival: Sheri and Gabe owe their lives to the four men who didn't hesitate to help them through an extreme mountainside rescue effort. If they hadn't been pulled back up to the road so quickly where ambulances could get to them, Gabe probably wouldn't have survived. Even though they were out in the middle of nowhere, medics acted quickly. They got Gabe to the trauma center as fast as they could, working hard to keep him alive throughout the journey. If you're in trouble, you have to get someone's attention that you need help. This can be easier said than done in some cases, but you can't give up. People are almost always willing to help if they see that you're in trouble.

The 12-Year-Old with a Million-to-One Chance

How long do you think you would survive by yourself in an African wildlife preserve that has over 1,500 lions roaming in it? Oh yeah, there's also hippos, leopards, cheetahs, rhinoceros, and elephants. Not interested in giving that a try? I don't blame you! But young Alex Mboweni found himself in just such a life-or-death situation.

Kruger National Park is a giant preserve that borders several countries in the southern part of Africa. It covers nearly 5 million acres. African wildlife is thriving there. That's some pretty deadly wildlife, by the way. Lions don't mess around. You don't want to be wandering around out there on foot, especially when the sun goes down and everything starts hunting.

One of the countries that borders the park is Mozambique. Mozambique is one of the poorest countries in the world. Each month, police catch about 3,000 people trying to sneak into the country of South Africa through Kruger National Park. Most of them come from Zimbabwe and Mozambique. It's a big problem. Most of these people are desperate for a better life and they feel like their best chance is to sneak into South Africa.

That's what Alex and his family were doing. Alex was 12 years old. Park guards saw the group of people sneaking across the border and chased them. The people split up and hid. Alex's mom was caught but didn't tell the police that her son was out there. She said that she was too scared. It would have been much better if she had told them to go look for Alex but she didn't. Alex was lost and alone.

That first night Alex was really scared. He was by himself and could hear lions roaring and lots of animals making noises and moving around. It got cold when the sun went down so he found an ant mound and laid against it to keep warm. This was smart. The ants left him alone. Ant and termite mounds in Africa can grow as high as 30 feet. They keep the ants cool during the day and warm at night. That night they kept Alex warm, too.

He spent the first two days without water. He wouldn't be able to keep that up. He couldn't find any. Without water, he would not stay alive for much longer. Luckily, he came across a river. He was very weak by this point but kept walking in the hope that he would find water. He found a lot of it.

Fortunately, there weren't any crocodiles in this river and Alex was able to drink. But as he was, an elephant charged him and ran him off. He found another ant mound to sleep on and would go to the river to drink every day, but each day he got weaker and weaker. He had not found any food, but at least he hadn't become food for any of the many animals that would have seen him as a meal.

Alex's father was living in South Africa and became worried when his wife and Alex hadn't shown up. He went to the police and told them that Alex was lost somewhere. The police found Alex's mom and took her to where she had been captured. They went up a hill and she yelled for Alex.

Alex had been lost for an astounding *eight days*. That's a really long time to be without food and not be found by a hungry lion. By this point, Alex didn't even have the strength to go down to the river to get water. He knew that he was dying. When he heard his mother's voice, he thought he was either dreaming or already dead.

The police thought this was crazy. There's no way they were going to find this kid after he had been missing for so long, not in a place as dangerous as this. But Alex shocked everyone when he walked out of the bushes.

Alex said, "After eight days I was too weak to walk to the river and I lost all hope. But then I heard the voice of my mother calling my name. The voices echoed down the rivers and the valleys so I managed to get closer to where I heard the voice calling my name and it was real, it was my mother calling me."

Alex was rushed to a nearby hospital where doctors and nurses looked after him for a week after nearly starving and dying of dehydration. That's one brave and lucky kid!

Keys to Survival: Once Alex found water, he stayed where he was, and that's a good thing. He could have wandered further away out of earshot from where the police and his family searched for him. Water is the most important thing to have if you're lost in the wilderness. Seeking the warmth of the ant mounds really helped him, too. It took a lot of toughness and courage to stay alive as long as Alex did all by himself.

A 16-Year-Old Alone in One of the Most Remote Places on Earth

One thing that makes any sailor's blood run cold is the thought of a rogue wave. Young Abby Sunderland was facing this unimaginable terror by herself at night in extremely remote waters. She was basically 2,000 miles from anywhere in the Indian Ocean. When darkness suddenly blots out the light of the moon, that can mean one of the scariest things on the planet is coming for you. A wave in the dead of the night that is so tall, it towers above everything on the horizon. She couldn't see it in the dark, but it was coming.

Abby was born into an adventurous, sailing family. Her older brother, Zac, had held the record for the youngest person to sail around the world by themselves for 42 days before it was broken. If Abby completed her journey around the world successfully, she would be the new record holder at 16 years old. She would set out from California where she had lived all her life. She was determined and felt up for the enormous challenge.

Sailing around the world is extremely risky. There's a lot that can go wrong, but Abby felt prepared. She set off into the South Pacific. When she went around the southern tip of South America, Cape Horn, she became the youngest person to do it alone. That itself was quite the feat! Cape Horn is so dangerous that it's known as "the graveyard of the sea." She had been sailing for two months at this point. That's a really long time to be by yourself, but so far, so good.

She made it to Africa after another month crossing the Atlantic. She was doing great although the autopilot system on her 40 foot sailboat was malfunctioning. She stopped in Cape Town, South Africa to get it fixed. It didn't take long before she was back at sea. Abby was a girl on a mission.

Leaving Africa behind, she set off across the Indian Ocean. She reached the middle of the Indian Ocean after four months at sea. She had sailed 12,000 miles! This is a desolate place. Sailing across these waters puts you halfway between Antarctica and India. Abby was 2,000 miles from Australia and 2,000 miles from Africa, right at the halfway point. It is truly the middle of nowhere.

This part of the Indian Ocean can be extremely treacherous for sailors. The water is cold and the weather is unpredictable and often really terrible. It can be very difficult to stay on course in this remote part of the world. Unfortunately for Abby, she would get to know how dangerous it is better than anyone.

Storms began to pummel Abby's boat one after the other. The waves were 45 feet tall. The winds were nearly 70 miles per hour. This was as terrifying a situation as you can experience alone at sea. The boat was getting knocked over, then it would right itself only to get knocked over again. The radar got knocked off of the mast which was Abby's communication to the outside world. She stayed calm and kept working.

Abby had been working to keep her sailboat upright for hours now. She was exhausted and struggling. Any sailor would have been in this mess. That's when disaster struck. A rogue wave that had been stirred up by the huge storm struck. It lifted the boat up and up and up. There was nothing that Abby could do. Finally, the boat began to roll. Abby crashed into the wall inside the boat and was knocked out as the freezing water came pouring in.

The mast of Abby's boat stood 60 feet tall. It snapped right off leaving the boat completely at the mercy of the storm now. Abby woke up to the horror of her situation. She kept a clear head somehow and set off the emergency distress beacons. This sent her location to ocean rescue centers all around the world and meant one thing. It notified everyone that Abby was in big, BIG trouble. She needed rescue and she needed it now.

Abby had been sailing for 138 days. Now she was drifting with all communication cut off. How long would it take rescuers to get to her location 2,000 miles from anywhere? A search plane set out from Australia. Abby was so far away that it wouldn't have much time to attempt to spot her before having to turn around or risk running out of fuel. But it found her. That's when rescuers knew that the boat's mast was broken. They were able to talk to Abby by radio because they were so close and she was able to tell them that she wasn't hurt.

Abby's family was overjoyed to hear that she was okay. They had been incredibly worried. It took 20 hours from the time she deployed the distress signal to the airplane locating her. After the search plane found her, three ships were sent to save her. One was a French ship that was 400 miles away. The ship's captain was Paul Louis Le Moigne. The weather was still bad when they reached Abby. As Paul Louis and the rest of his men launched a raft to go get Abby, the captain was knocked into the frigid waves and was lucky to get back into the raft.

The crew bravely got over to Abby's boat and got her aboard and safely to the larger boat. It was a dramatic rescue. Abby and her parents got a lot of criticism over her rescue. Many people thought that she was too young to try something so dangerous. But some experienced sailors defended her saying that she didn't need to be rescued because of bad decisions but because of bad luck. A random rogue wave can get anyone no matter how experienced they are.

Abby was lucky to be alive but performed admirably in her attempt to sail around the world by herself as a 16-year-old. Even though she failed and her adventure was ridiculed by many, she also earned the respect of those who truly knew the sea and the dangers of sailing.

Keys to Survival: Abby remained calm and remembered her training. If the boat is helpless or damaged, the only option was to deploy the distress beacons and wait. She was lucky that her boat wasn't broken in half and sunk. She had a life raft ready if that happened. She was prepared for anything. And when going on a dangerous adventure, you'd better be!

Avalanche!

It was a beautiful morning on the slopes. The resort had gotten over a foot of fresh snow the night before and skiers were excited. It's a real joy for snow skiers when there is a bunch of fresh powder to ski. Ken Scott was at the Idaho resort early. Rebecca Hurlen-Patano was there, too. They were both regulars at the resort slopes called Silver Mountain. There's nothing quite like making fresh tracks in brand new snow.

They set off together and it was amazing skiing conditions. After a few runs, they saw that the 16-to-1 trail was open. That was exciting. It hadn't been open yet that season due to avalanche fears. It was an advanced trail. As soon as the sun rose over the mountain, a safety team had detonated more than a dozen explosives up on the trail to knock off loose snow and lower the chances of an avalanche. Surely, those explosions would have caused an avalanche if there was going to be one today, so the trail was opened.

Ken and Rebecca headed up there and met several other Silver Mountain regulars on the way. Rebecca looked at Ken and grinned. She started down the trail. As soon as she did, it happened. Rebecca yelled, "Avalanche!" But the giant slabs of snow were sliding and falling and took all of the skiers with them. In an avalanche, you're supposed to do everything you can to stay up on top of the snow as it carries you. You want your head to be as close to the surface as possible when it all stops. Ken tried his best, but this avalanche was too powerful. He was completely at the mercy of the snow.

Rebecca found herself 500 feet from where the avalanche had picked her up. But she wasn't stuck too far below the surface of the snow and was able to punch her way out. She started yelling for the other skiers. Ken was only 10 feet up the slope from her and poked his ski pole up out of the snow in response. He was much more buried than Rebecca had been but he wasn't terribly deep. He couldn't move much, but he could breathe. Rebecca found two of the other three skiers that had been on the slope with them and they were buried but alive and breathing. She couldn't find the fifth. She knew that if they were knocked out and buried, they might suffocate. Or they might be awake but too buried to breathe. She had to work quickly.

Ken was okay, so Rebecca went down the slope a little to help the others. One skier only had his head sticking out of the snow so she started to dig him out. That's when she heard it. There was a massive explosion that meant a *second* avalanche! She didn't even have time to turn around before the wall of snow hit her. This avalanche was even bigger than the first one, but Rebecca was lucky. She wasn't buried badly by this one either. In fact, most of the snow passed over her after knocking her another 20 feet down the slope.

Ken heard the roar of the second avalanche too. And he knew it meant that he was a dead man. Before, he could see up out of where he was buried. Now there was only darkness. Another nine feet of snow had been dumped on top of him. He was in really big trouble now. It would be hard to find him and only a matter of time before he ran out of air. He couldn't move at all with all the new snow pressing down on him. It was even hard to breathe because he could barely expand his lungs. That's seriously stuck!

As Rebecca climbed out of the snow for a second time, her heart sank. Everything looked different. She had no idea where the other skiers were now. There were big mounds of snow everywhere that hadn't been there just moments earlier. How would she possibly find everyone again?

Meanwhile, Ken was trying not to panic. He didn't want to die. Suffocation is a slow death. You have plenty of time to think about your life and all the things that you would do if you only had more time. Ken thought about his family and tried to focus. Nobody heard him scream.

Rebecca still had her phone and called in reinforcements. In just 10 minutes, there were 50 rescuers on the mountain slope helping Rebecca try to find the buried skiers. They had to be fast. Most victims of avalanches die from running out of air, buried underneath the snow. They brought shovels and tent poles for probing into the snow. Rebecca directed them to where she guessed her friends were.

The rescuers spaced out evenly in a line. They would poke down into the snow with the tent poles hoping to hit a buried skier. Then they would all take a step and try again. After 40 minutes, they hit something! They had found a skier named Bill Fuzak, and although unconscious, he was still alive. This helped Rebecca get her bearings. She knew that Ken was about 20 feet up the slope from Bill.

Usually, rescuers have 30 minutes to save someone buried by an avalanche. Ken knew that he was past that point. If he was going to die, he wanted to get on with it. In the darkness, he had begun to feel warm. That could only mean one thing. Hypothermia. This is what happens when your body temperature gets too low. Ken was feeling warm because his blood was flowing to the core of his body to protect those organs. He knew that he would be dead soon.

Then he felt something. Ouch. Was that a probe? He didn't feel it again and started to get really sad. That may have been his only chance. The rescuer must not have felt him. Minutes passed. The rescuers had moved on. But then the snow above him started to shake. They were digging him out and 5 minutes later he was gulping in the air through the hole that the rescuers had dug. It felt great when his arms were finally free. He grabbed Rebecca and hugged her tight. They were both so happy but Rebecca through her smile told him to let go of her, he still needed to get to a hospital! Ken said that he couldn't, he was too happy and grateful to let go.

Keys to Survival: Ken had been trained in avalanche survival. He did his best to "swim" to the top of the snow as it carried him down the mountain but that can be hard to do. You don't want to find yourself upside down in the snow. You want to end up with your head not far from the surface with your arm or arms up in order to have a chance to free yourself. Once buried, Ken took really small breaths to try and not run out of air too quickly before he was rescued. He was also able to avoid panicking which makes you use more air.

Falling 29,000 Feet
Without a Parachute

This adventurer millionaire was certainly determined. He desperately wanted to be the first person to fly all the way around the world in a hot air balloon by himself. On his 4th attempt, he found himself plunging from 29,000 feet up in the sky with his balloon in tatters. Below him was the murky shark-infested water of the Coral Sea.

Steve Fossett is one of history's fascinating characters. He became a millionaire in the finance industry and then dedicated his life to breaking records. He held records as a pilot, sailor, and balloonist. He set over 100 records in his lifetime and they were in five different fields of adventure. His accomplishments are simply incredible. He had a seemingly fearless approach to how he lived life.

Steve had gone more than 15,000 miles, two thirds of the way around the world, when he ran into trouble. Actually, the first sign of trouble happened on the first day when he realized that he forgot to bring toilet paper. Yuck! But he ran into serious trouble after he'd crossed over Australia. A fierce storm hit. Storms are obviously dangerous for balloonists for a number of reasons.

They can force the balloon up too high for a person to breathe. Steve had heaters in his balloon with him because at 29,000 feet, it's REALLY cold. Another problem is the wind, as well as lightning strikes. But what doomed this flight for Steve was hail.

Fast-falling ice is bad enough for planes but for a hot air balloon? Deadly. The balloon got shredded by the flying balls of ice. But this was a unique hot air balloon. It was 150 feet tall. And it had two balloon compartments. The larger one was full of helium. That got destroyed by the hail and down Steve started. He still had a smaller balloon compartment that was full of hot air. Even though he was falling fast, it wasn't as if he had jumped out of an airplane without a parachute. Now that I think about it, a parachute may have been even more useful to him than the missing toilet paper!

Steve didn't expect to live as he fell, but he jumped into action to give himself the best chance. He started throwing out everything heavy like the extra fuel tanks. He put as much power as he could into the tanks heating the air in the hot air compartment that was left. Steve fell into the sea at 45 miles per hour. That could have easily killed him, but that is a slower speed than a skydiver falls. A skydiver falls at 120 miles per hour. The compartment of hot air that had remained intact saved his life.

When he hit the water, he was still in danger. Amazingly, he wasn't even injured when he hit, but his capsule was on fire and then started to fill with water. He said, "I was very surprised, I thought it would kill me. In just the last 30 seconds I cut away a lot of tanks. Maybe I gave the balloon a little bit of lift so

I hit the water more gently, and then the capsule was immediately pulled underwater and filled with water."

Steve grabbed both a distress beacon and the life raft. They were the two things that he absolutely had to have. He then swam into the chilly waters to escape the fiery capsule. He floated there for 10 hours before the rescue boats were able to find him. He wasn't too scared to try to fly around the world two more times! Finally, on his 6th attempt, he made it all the way around the world. He was 58 but not finished with his crazy adventures. He never would be.

Keys to Survival: Even though he didn't have a parachute (or toilet paper), Steve was prepared for a sea landing. He had both a distress beacon which would let rescuers know where he was and he had an inflatable life raft on board. He must have been really surprised to be alive when he crashed down, but he still had to act quickly and not panic. Even with his capsule on fire and filling up with water, he grabbed the two items essential for his survival. And in the shark-infested waters 500 miles off the Australian coast, you definitely want to be in a raft and not all the way in the water!

Shipwrecked & Sold Into Slavery

The fog was so thick that the men couldn't see anything. Then they felt the unmistakable crash of hitting rocks. The year was 1815 and Captain James Riley's merchant ship crashed into the rocks along the coast of northern Africa near what is modern-day Morocco. What happened next is a harrowing story of survival.

The men got their wooden rowboat ready now that their ship was doomed. They were in hostile territory. James Riley was an American from Connecticut and had been sailing all his life. Now he was involved in trade and was sailing from Gibraltar to the Cape Verde Islands when he became shipwrecked. There were a total of 11 men aboard the boat.

That number went to 10 men pretty quickly. Two natives killed one of the men as the rest made their escape. They drifted in the rowboat for 9 days. They had run out of food and water, so they headed for land. It was an unforgiving place they found. The Sahara desert sprawls across most of northern Africa and extends all along the coast of where James and his men found themselves.

They had tried to make it all the way out to the Cape Verde Islands in their rowboat but the islands were too far and the waves were too big. They had no choice but to try their luck with the natives. They hoped that they might find a tribe that was friendly. It wasn't long before they had been captured by the nomadic Oulad Bou Sbaa people. James and his men would almost regret not dying at sea.

Their captors took them as slaves and treated them brutally. They were not given water or food and forced to work and march through the desert without any clothes. Their skin became terribly burnt. They were forced to drink camel urine to survive. They lost so much weight that they looked like skeletons. James went from 275 pounds down to 90. They were starving and terribly dehydrated. Several of the men were sold to other groups of nomads and never seen again. Typically slaves would be worked to death and in the Sahara Desert, that usually didn't take too long.

James was able to learn a good bit of the nomads' language. When two traders arrived, Sidi Hamet and his brother, James was able to convince them to buy him and his three remaining crewmen who were still with him. James said that if they took them the hundreds of miles to the nearest city, a friend would pay Sidi a nice ransom for them. Sidi liked the sound of that but told James that if he was lying, he would kill him. James didn't have a friend in that city but would worry about that later. He knew he would die if he stayed where he was.

As James and his men clung to the camels they rode, they at least had some hope for the first time since their capture. It was still a terrifying journey.

Miraculously, they made it 300 miles to a city in Morocco.

Sidi took a note that James had written into town. James had addressed it to the American consul in the long-shot hope that he would help him. His life depended on it. Sidi met a man who worked for a British merchant who served as England's consul in the city. James' letter finding this man was a small miracle. He was William Willshire, and he was so moved by the letter that he was eager to help save the enslaved Americans.

William rode out to where James and his men were being held in the outskirts of the city and met them with tears and hugs. William said, "Welcome to my arms, my dear sir, this is truly a happy moment!" He paid Sidi his money and James was saved. He would see his wife and 5 children again.

It took the men some time to recover from their ordeal, but eventually, they were well enough to travel back to the United States. James would even found a town in Ohio that he named, Willshire, in gratitude to the man who saved his life. He would also write a bestselling book about his experience as a Saharan slave. Abraham Lincoln read it and considered it one of the most important books in the world. It deeply influenced how the future president felt about slavery, which means that Captain James Riley's incredible survival played a small role in the abolishment of slavery in America.

TWO Great White Sharks Hunting a 15-Year-Old Kid

Sharks are super scary to most of us. Some people can't think of anything that's scarier! Sure, we can read about how we have a greater chance of being struck by lightning than being attacked by a shark, but somehow it doesn't seem to help much. Especially when you're swimming in the ocean. Who would be more scared of lightning? Lightning doesn't sneakily glide through dark water underneath you or have huge sharp teeth. There might not be a more terrifying predator on earth than the Great White Shark. But what about TWO Great White Sharks?

Shannon Ainslie had just gone back to his 9th grade classrooms after Christmas break. After that first day back to school, he wanted to have some fun. So he met up with his friends and his brother and they hit the beach at Nahoon Reef. Shannon lived in South Africa which is known for its great surfing...and its Great White Sharks. It was a warm day and the nice waves were too inviting to pass up.

It's conventional wisdom for South African surfers to not go in the water if it smells fishy or if they see birds diving into the water catching fish. Those two things usually mean that something else is hunting fish...sharks. The boys had been having lots of fun for

almost two hours. It was then that Shannon's brother and his friends got out. They picked up a slight smell of sardines in the water and that made them nervous. Sardines are very tasty to sharks.

Shannon and a few others decided to stay in and at first, he was glad he did. He saw the perfect wave approaching. He hadn't gotten a big one all day but here it was. He paddled hard and was just about to pop up on his board when it happened.

Shannon had no idea what was happening at first. One second he was completely focused on catching the wave and the next? He had been hit hard by something big. He was suddenly knocked up into the air, and it was a cold-blooded killer that did it. The Great White Shark attacking him bit down, catching both Shannon's hand and his surfboard in its mouth. The great beast quickly dragged him under the water. Just as it did, Shannon saw *ANOTHER* Great White with its jaws open, aiming right for his head.

The shark that had him already, yanked him just out of reach of the other shark that barely missed chomping down on his head. Strangely, each shark saved him from the other one. The first shark must have been startled by the second shark, so it let go of Shannon's hand. When it did, Shannon felt the pain of the bite for the first time and everything slowed down. People in near-death situations describe this a lot. Everything happening around you seems to slow and you become hyper-aware of each second as it slowly passes.

Shannon found himself under the clear water of Nahoon Reef staring that Great White Shark right in the face, practically nose to nose. Here's the scary thing. The shark had its mouth wide open! It was the first shark that had bitten his hand and Shannon thought it must have been as surprised as he was by everything that had just happened. The two just stayed right there, motionless, staring at each other. The 15-foot Great White, seemingly frozen, with its mouth wide open and ready to strike, and the 9th grader looking death right in its cold black eye. Shannon thought it must have been confused because it just sat there staring at him.

I hope you don't have nightmares about this. I hope I don't either! But as long as we don't go surfing at Nahoon Reef, we should both be okay and avoid experiencing a situation like this. After their stare-down, the huge shark abruptly darted past Shannon. It felt like he was shoved forward by the monster and he quickly swam to the surface as soon as it passed.

Thankfully, Shannon's board was right there in front of him. He hopped up on it and it got him out of the water despite the giant bite mark on it. It was then that he noticed his hand. It was barely attached to his arm. The shark nearly bit it clean off. That's really gross, I know. To make matters worse, there were no waves (or other surfers) to help Shannon back to shore. The other surfers had abandoned him and the waves suddenly died, leaving him more than 300 feet from shore with at least two hungry Great Whites close by.

Shannon was in shock and overcome with fear and panic. He had heard about sharks circling back to finish someone off after the first attack. Terror washed over him. He'd never make it that far back to the beach by himself with one hand and one of these giant killers could get him at any second. Just then, a good-sized wave came out of nowhere and Shannon was able to coast on it for a bit toward the shore. But no more waves came and it took him another 20 minutes to paddle all the way to safety. That must have seemed like 2 hours. In most shark attack stories, people selflessly swim and rescue the attack victim. That didn't happen for Shannon.

When he finally got to the beach, he was losing a lot of blood from his wound and it hurt terribly. Someone grabbed the surfboard leg rope and used it as a tourniquet to slow the bleeding. His brother hurried him to the hospital where his fingers were sewn back together and his hand was reattached.

Amazingly, Shannon remained dedicated to surfing. He somehow became *less* scared of sharks after his attack. He started his own surf school teaching the sport to others. When he grew up, he moved nearly 9,000 miles to Norway to be an instructor for the country's national surf team. Norway is about as far from South Africa as you can get. And I think that was a really good move as the Great White Shark has never been seen in the waters around Norway. There's never even been a fatal shark attack in Norway...ever. So if you ever try surfing, maybe do it there!

Keys to Survival: First things first, I want to start by putting you at ease, or at least trying to. Last year, there were only 73 shark attacks on people in the entire world. Out of 8 billion people, only 73 were attacked by a shark. And only 9 of those were fatal. Shark attacks are extremely rare. This is especially true if you avoid swimming near the mouths of rivers where they meet the ocean, or anywhere people are fishing, like a pier. The early morning and the evening are the most common times that sharks accidentally bite someone. The main way that people have survived shark attacks is by fighting back with all your strength. This includes jabbing at its eyes or gills or simply kicking and punching wherever you can. For Shannon, the key to survival was that he had to find the courage and the strength to get all the way back to the safety of the beach by himself. Oftentimes, a shark will attack and then swim around waiting for its victim to die. If you're not dead after an attack, all you have to do is get to shore and you won't be attacked again. If you're losing blood from a wound, you need to find something to use as a tourniquet to slow down the bleeding once you are on shore. Since Shannon's wound was on his hand, the cord was wrapped tightly around his upper arm which slowed blood flow down the arm. It's important to keep as much blood as possible where it belongs... inside your body!

9-Year-Old Attacked
by FOUR Pit Bulls

There are two sides to the issue of pit bulls. This is a breed of dog that (according to some studies) is involved in 60-70% of all dog attacks. They are extremely strong dogs and can be deadly. They tend not to release their bite once they latch on to an attack victim, and because of the strength of their jaws, this can cause a lot of damage.

There are many who defend pit bulls such as Cesar Millan, the "Dog Whisperer". He is one of the world's most famous dog trainers and he loves pit bulls. He says that they are not naturally vicious. But some cities such as Miami and Denver have made it against the law to have a pit bull.

I don't know enough to say who is right and who is wrong on the issue of pit bulls. It is true that other breeds of dogs are involved in attacks on people, too. This is a very scary experience and people every year are killed in dog attacks. This is the story of an attack of a 9-year-old girl who is extremely lucky to be alive.

Angie Hands was walking home from school that day just like she did every day. She lived in Tijeras, New Mexico, just outside of Albuquerque. Angie's uncle had four pit bulls. The two young ones had escaped their fence and as poor Angie walked by, they attacked. Nobody knows why this happened. We know that Angie didn't do anything wrong to provoke the attack. As the two dogs lunged at her, the two parent dogs climbed a six foot fence to join them and descended on the helpless girl.

One dog can kill a person, but Angie had the misfortune to be attacked by four of them. Most people would tell you that there's no way that a 9-year-old would survive that. It's a miracle that Angie did. She found herself on a rescue helicopter whisking her to the University of New Mexico Burn and Trauma Center. She went into surgery quickly. She was barely hanging on to life. Her surgery would last an astonishing 30 hours.

The good news is that she lived through that helicopter ride and the surgery. The bad news was that she would need decades of surgeries. Angie was lucky that the dogs did not attack her neck, head, or face. She was also lucky that they didn't attack her torso or do damage to any of her major organs. But she might have to have her arms and legs amputated. Her mother fought hard to get the doctors to try everything they could to save her limbs and amazingly, they did.

Angie was in the trauma center for more than two months. It took a team of almost 80 nurses and doctors, all working together to save her. That includes everyone from the nurse in the helicopter to the chief surgeon. On the day that Angie went home, they all took a picture in front of the helicopter. The entire staff of the trauma center stood there smiling with their brave patient, the miracle girl who had survived the impossible.

The doctors and nurses were amazing and helped in more ways than saving Angie's life and her arms and legs. She also had to accept that her body would be covered in scars for the rest of her life. Angie grew into a well adjusted, confident, and successful woman. It has been 38 years since the attack happened on that normal afternoon in 1984.

On the 30th anniversary of the attack, Angie went on a 30 mile bike ride. She did it to celebrate not just being alive, but having the legs to use to ride a bike. She is reminded of her attack every day by her scars. Every day she feels grateful to all of the people who helped to save her. She also tracked down the main group of people who helped her so much, but there was one that she couldn't find. It was nurse Laura who called her "Angie Boo." Angie never forgot her, but she didn't know her last name and hadn't seen her in 31 years. She posted about nurse Laura on Facebook in the hopes that she could be reconnected to tell Laura how much she still meant to her.

Laura had moved from New Mexico up to Seattle, Washington a few years after caring for Angie in the 80s. She was still a nurse and thought often about the brave little girl that she had helped all those years ago. She didn't know that girl was looking for her, and she didn't know that little girl also lived in the Seattle area!

Angie still had a photograph of nurse Laura by her bedside from 1984. When someone tracked down

Laura and told Angie that she had found her, Angie was overjoyed. She cried because she was so happy.

Laura was really happy too. She said, "This is so crazy, I've thought about Angie for years. My family has heard the story. I can picture what she looked like, her little haircut." She went on to say that, "It's a pretty amazing feeling knowing that you can make such a difference in someone's life and not realize it." She had no idea that Angie credited her for giving her the confidence and courage to start living again.

Then, one day Angie happened to have a TV turned on and heard a voice that gave her goosebumps. It was the voice of a camp counselor that she met two years after the attack. Other kids were being cruel about her scars and messed up arms. This camp counselor told her that her scars didn't matter. It's who you are on the inside that counts. Angie never forgot that lesson. That camp counselor (Joline Gutierrez Krueger) now worked for a newspaper and Angie was able to track her down also and thank her for the impact that she had on her life. All because she recognized her voice on television, more than 30 years later!

Keys to Survival: Angie survived because she was quickly gotten to highly skilled doctors who worked fast to save her. There are things that you can do to give yourself the best chance of surviving a dog attack. You don't want to run. That will trigger a chase response in a dog. Don't look the dog in the eyes. If the dog attacks, you want to give it things to bite instead of you like a backpack, bag, jacket, etc. If you have a bicycle, try to keep it between you and the dog. If you get knocked down or fall, curl up in a ball and put your hands around the back of your neck and your arms and elbows over your face and ears. Don't yell or scream and try to be as still as you can. That advice is easier said than done in the heat of the moment, but experts agree that stillness and playing dead is the most effective strategy.

Plummeting Into Icy Darkness

He just wanted coffee. No big deal. He'll just walk out, scoop up some ice, and take it back to the tent to melt it. John All was a scientist studying the effects of pollution in the Himalayan Mountains. He was a Western Kentucky University professor and avid mountain climber. He'd even climbed up Mount Everest before. He was experienced, but he was alone. His climbing partners had just left because one of them was feeling ill. They'd be back in a couple of days so John decided to stay. He wouldn't venture far. He was 20,000 feet up on Mount Himlung in Nepal. But he'd stay close to his tent. He'd be fine...as long as he had coffee.

He walked over to a patch of fresh snow about 50 feet from his tent. He had his crampons on his boots. Those are spikes that help your boots grip the snow. Yep, that looks like good snow to melt for coffee. Then he was falling...into darkness.

John had been camped right next to a completely hidden and very deep crevasse. Crevasses are cracks in glacier ice that can be hundreds of feet deep. They're hidden killers for mountain climbers when they get covered up with snow. John tried his best to save his life. He had ice axes in his hands and he tried to stick one into the wall as he fell, but he only succeeded in ripping his arm out of the socket. He kept on falling.

He crashed into something and felt immense pain. He had fallen 70 feet. That's like falling off the roof of a 7-story building. He was lucky to be alive. It took a bit to realize just how lucky. He had fallen into the crevasse right above a big chunk of ice that had also fallen in. Below that chunk of ice was only darkness, and John's legs were dangling over the abyss. Landing on that ice had kept him from falling perhaps hundreds more feet to his death.

He was in bad shape. Falling 70 feet is enough to kill you. John couldn't move and was in terrible pain. It hurt to breathe. He had 15 bones that were broken. His ribs were fractured into pieces. Six of the vertebrae in his spine were smashed. John knew that he was bleeding internally and that he probably had several internal organs that were badly injured. He only had one arm left to work with, as the other hung limp at his side. This might be the end, he thought. It was so cold down there.

If he was still down in this crevasse when night fell, there would be no climbing out. He would freeze to death if he spent the night there. He had crampons on and one ice ax. He saw that the crevasse narrowed in one direction which meant that maybe there was a chance of climbing up over there. If it got narrow enough to put his back against the ice on one side and he could reach the other wall with his feet, maybe he could climb out.

But to get over there meant that he had to climb on a wall of ice over the deep drop into nothingness...

with one arm, and a broken body. But there were other chunks of ice or ledges that he could rest on where he would be safe. So off he went. He would spend around 15 minutes over the darkness of the abyss before getting to the next ice ledge. One wrong move meant falling and dying. Even though his body was so badly broken that it hurt to breathe, he made it. It took a remarkable effort, but after hours of painful work, he climbed out of his icy grave.

John was worn out. He had no energy left. He was much safer now that he was out of the crevasse and just minutes away from his tent but he couldn't walk. What should have taken a few minutes took hours of crawling. He hadn't had any water all day. If only he had gotten his coffee that morning! When he finally crawled back into his tent, he couldn't get his water bottle open with just one working arm.

In the tent was John's satellite phone. He couldn't make calls but could make a Facebook post. He managed to type, "Please call Global Rescue. John broken arm, ribs, internal bleeding. Fell 70 ft crevasse. Climbed out. Himlung camp 2, Please hurry." He hoped that someone would see it. It was only four o'clock in the morning back home. He needed rescue NOW. He pulled his sleeping bag over his body and hoped that he would be alive in the morning.

John did wake up the next day. He could tell that the sky was getting lighter. Maybe he would make it. By now, he could hardly move. He was dying of thirst, the cold, and whatever organ damage he had.

Eighteen hours after climbing into the tent and laying down, he heard the helicopter. His friends had done it! They had gotten him rescued. A man unzipped his tent and popped his head in, happy to see him still breathing. As John was flying down the mountain in the helicopter, he knew that he would be okay.

Keys to Survival: John's survival was incredibly unlikely. He became only the 2nd person to fall that far into a crevasse and live. John's survival was unlikely because he was alone. He made that unfortunate decision not to go with his climbing partners down the mountain. He survived by sheer determination and his incredible ice climbing skill. Nobody knew he was in trouble, which is dangerous. He hadn't grabbed his satellite phone because he was not walking far. John thought about the people he loved and that kept him from giving up.

Lost in the Biggest Desert on Earth

He knew he was going to die. He had tried his best, but he had no water. He was completely lost in the biggest desert in the world. He used charcoal to write a goodbye note to his family and laid down. He didn't expect to wake up.

The Sahara Desert covers 3.6 million square miles in northern Africa. During the summer, it is the hottest place in the world. Its average summer temperature is over 100 degrees. Clouds or rain are basically nonexistent. To survive here, you have to be ready for unrelenting and merciless sunshine. Pack your sunscreen! Oh, and the never-ending sun heats up the sand to 176 degrees. You sure don't want to be caught barefoot! There's not much animal life beyond sand vipers, lizards, and the *deathstalker* scorpion. That's seriously what it's called, which is quite fitting as pretty much everything in the Sahara will kill you.

Sounds like a great place to go on vacation, doesn't it? It actually attracts its share of explorers and adventurists. There is a 155-mile foot race called the Marathon des Sables, which is French for Marathon of the Sands. As you might imagine, it is only for the most extreme runner. It's been going on for more than 35 years and is known as the most difficult foot race on the planet. It takes place in southern Morocco and attracts more runners than you might think. Some years the race has nearly 1,000 participants.

Now I'll introduce you to this story's hero, Mauro Prosperi. Mauro was Italian and had worked as a police officer before he became an Olympic pentathlete. He could really run and a desert race sounded interesting to him. He went in 2004 and that year there were only 86 runners. Mauro's wife was rightfully worried about him entering this crazy race. He assured her that all he had to worry about was getting a sunburn. It was his first run in a desert but he felt prepared. He was going with a friend. He wasn't too worried, even though each runner had to fill out a form with where to send their body if they died during the race!

The runners carried all of their supplies with them in a small backpack. They carried food, water, clothes, a compass, a sleeping bag, camping stove, and each runner had a signal flare in case they got lost. As they started, they stretched out in a long line with each runner going at their own pace. Everyone covered 60 miles over the first few days. By day four, the temperature was 115 degrees but Mauro was performing really well. He was in 4th place.

That's when the trouble began. Mauro was running by himself when the wind started to whip up. That's not a good thing in the desert. Without warning, he found himself in a sandstorm. The sand felt like needles hitting his face but if he stopped running, he was worried that he'd get buried! So he kept going...for *8 hours* through the sandstorm. Yikes! He wouldn't be in that race if he wasn't tough. He also kept running because even though he couldn't see very far at all, he felt as though he could see the trail.

It was almost night when the sand stopped blowing. And there was no trail. This was a problem. So was Mauro's bleeding face from getting pelted by sand for 8 hours. He stopped and rested for the night. When he woke, there was no wind at all. He figured it wouldn't take long to find the other runners. So he started to run and kept it up for 4 hours. But there was no sign of anyone. He climbed a really tall sand dune and looked all around. There was nothing but desert that looked exactly the same in every direction. Not good! To make matters worse, he was running really low on water. It was then that he remembered a story that his grandfather had told him from when he was a soldier at war and ran out of water. Mauro peed into a bottle in case he would have to drink it. Apparently, it worked for his grandfather. He would definitely need it.

Every runner had been told that if they get lost, stay put until rescuers find you. So that's what Mauro did for the rest of the day. It's too bad he hadn't done that 12 hours earlier. As the sun was going down, he saw it. There was a helicopter flying low over the dunes coming toward him. Rescue! He fired his signal flare into the air. But somehow the helicopter didn't see it and flew on. He was on his own for at least another night.

The next day he walked for hours. He didn't think that just sitting in the sun was the right approach.

Thankfully he came across a Muslim shrine. He thought there would be someone there to help him but it was abandoned. It was only used by desert nomads as they passed through. Nobody actually lived in it, but it made a good shelter for Mauro. He thought that all he had to do was stay alive and eventually someone would find him here. He stuck an Italian flag on the roof hoping that someone might see that. He licked the morning dew off of rocks and cooked up some dehydrated meals in his stove with...urine. Yum! His meals needed liquid to cook and that was all he had.

After several days he started to drink the urine directly to stay alive. He found bird eggs and ate lizards and beetles that he caught. The shrine had a tower on top that bats lived in. He ate those, too. He survived for 4 days like that when he heard a plane fly overhead. It didn't stop. He drew large SOS signs in the sand and started a little fire so that rescuers might see the smoke. But another sandstorm came along and ruined those plans.

He was surprised that he was still alive so he decided to keep moving. He would squeeze the roots of plants for drops of water and kept hunting lizards, snakes, and beetles as he walked. He ate them raw. He dug holes in the sand to sleep in at night to stay warm when the temperature dipped after the sun went down. He kept going in the same direction by keeping his path toward some distant mountains. After a couple of days, he came across a small oasis with a puddle of water that would save his life. He was in rough shape at this point. It had been 8 days since the sandstorm had caused him to get lost. He was extremely dehydrated and laid next to the puddle for the rest of the day taking small sips. The next day, he filled his bottles with the water and kept going.

That afternoon he saw fresh goat poop! He followed along looking for more poop and eventually came across human footprints. Then he saw a girl tending to a small herd of goats. He ran up to her and she ran away screaming. He thought he must look like a zombie. He did. He was just skin and bones and looked terrible. The girl came back with her grandmother and they helped him. Eventually, he was able to drink and eat, although it was hard at first. He was put on a camel and taken to a village where military police blindfolded him and questioned him, suspecting that he was a spy. Mauro found out that he had walked 180 miles into Algeria.

The police took him to a hospital where he was nursed back to life. His wife couldn't believe it when she got his phone call. Everyone had thought he had died. He was welcomed back to Italy as a hero. The race organizer couldn't believe that Mauro's story was possible. He called Mauro a liar and thought that he had been hiding out somewhere and made up the story to become famous. But his path was retraced and his incredible story was proven truthful.

Mauro didn't fully recover for two whole years after his survival. He probably wouldn't have lived another day out there. What did he do when he got better? He went right back to desert racing and competed in 8 more races. Would you still be desert racing if you had been stranded in the desert and nearly died?

Keys to Survival: Mauro was pushed to the limit of how long a person can survive in the desert without food or water. He was able to get some liquid from the reptiles and bats that he caught to eat. He was also forced to drink his own pee. This should only be done when there are no other options at all. It's not good for you to drink urine, but when you're lost in the desert it is extremely hard to find water. Mauro was very resourceful and able to find just enough to survive by squeezing water out of what few plants he came across and licking up morning dew. He was lucky to find the puddle in the oasis, as you can spend weeks in the Sahara without seeing an oasis. He was also lucky to find the goat shepherd as very few people live out there. Rescuers did end up finding the Muslim shrine that he stayed in so he probably would have been better off staying there. Fortunately, it worked out for him. I'm going to go drink a nice glass of ice water now.

I Was Just Minding
My Own Business...

You've probably heard about how to avoid being struck by lightning, and I know you've seen it. The sky lights up and you see the strike darting across the sky and then a few seconds later, the thunder crashes. Lightning is a fascinating thing. You just don't want to see it up close, or even worse...feel it. There was once a poor guy who was hit by lighting an astonishing FOUR times! Well, sort of...

Around 2,000 people die each year by being struck by lightning. That's a crazy way to die. Sometimes it's not that random and people could have taken precautions to avoid it. Other times? People were just minding their own business and the universe decided to zap them. Boom! Lightning strike.

The universe sure seemed like it was trying to kill Walter Summerford, but he was a survivor. Lightning strikes never could end his life, but they sure hurt. It all started when Walter was serving as a Major in the British Army. It was World War I, and Walter was in Belgium. As he was riding his horse across an open field, BAM! Poor Walter was not hit by a bullet, but by lightning!

It's not clear what happened to his horse, but Walter was paralyzed. He couldn't move his legs. He was no longer of any use to the army, so he retired. Eventually, feeling returned in his legs and he was able to walk again after a few months.

He moved to Canada. No longer in the army, he started a new life in a new country. Canada is a huge country and full of beautiful lakes, rivers, and streams. Walter picked up fishing as a hobby and six years after his misfortune in the Belgian field, he was zapped a second time in 1924.

Walter was relaxing by a river catching fish. He was sitting under a tree with his line in the water. It sounds like a peaceful scene doesn't it? Fortunately, Walter wasn't IN the water or he would have died. Lightning struck the tree he was sitting under and got him, too. This time it wasn't a direct hit, but it still got him good. The right side of his body was paralyzed this time. He did well to go get some help with just one side of his body working. It took nearly two years, but once again Walter regained feeling in his right arm and leg and was able to fully recover. He must have been pretty spooked after his second encounter with lightning.

Some people would never go outside again after being hit twice by electric bolts out the sky. But not Walter. He was an outdoorsman. He worked hard in his rehabilitation to be able to walk again. He loved being outside and walking around in the great outdoors. There's no way this poor guy would get struck by lightning a third time, right?

Wrong. Six years passed...again. It was 1930 and Walter was taking a stroll through a park near his home. Incredibly, it happened AGAIN. But this time was the worst of all of them. Walter was completely paralyzed from the neck down. Still, he survived. Was he the unluckiest man in the world? It sure seemed that way.

Unfortunately, this time Walter would not get the feeling back in his limbs. He lived the next two years in a hospital bed before he died. It was a tragic ending for a man who loved being outdoors. Doctors couldn't believe that he lived through three lightning strikes. Walter was a fighter. He was tough. He bravely hung on after that third strike but it was just too much.

His story didn't end there. Here's where it gets even more interesting. This might be the most extraordinary thing about this story. Four years after Walter died (yes, that's six years after his third encounter with lighting), lightning struck his tombstone and split it in half. SERIOUSLY? The year was 1936.

I know this seems far fetched, but this really happened. Walter had been buried in Vancouver where he had lived since moving from England. His final resting place was the Mountain View Cemetery. Because Walter was strangely struck by lightning every six years (even after he was dead), his family felt that he must have been the victim of a curse or witchcraft. It was spooky and didn't make much scientific sense. The odds of being struck just three times are nearly impossible. The life of Walter Summerford is extremely strange and fascinating.

Keys to Survival: The best way to survive a lightning strike is to avoid them entirely! Surprisingly, only one out of every ten people that get struck by lighting actually die. Most people survive. Your chances of being hit by lighting are around 1 in 70,000. That's really low. Those odds get even better if you're smart about not playing in thunderstorms. Even if the storm seems far away, it's a great idea to get out of a pool or body of water. Don't take a shower or bath during a thunderstorm. You don't want to be close to any body of water. If you see a lightning strike, get inside and don't ever take shelter underneath a tree. Tall things tend to get hit. It's better to get rained on than to be under a tree. If you're close to something that gets hit by lightning, you can also get zapped through the ground. It's best to just wait out a thunderstorm inside your house!

Farmer Takes Extreme
Action to Save Himself

Those 3,000 hogs weren't going to feed themselves. The 1,500 acres of fields weren't going to take care of themselves either. Farming is hard work. Really hard! But Kurt Kaser is one tough dude. He had grown up on his farm, right there in the corner of Nebraska, not far from the Iowa border. Now he was 63, and he had been running the farm for a long time, just like his dad and grandad did before him.

Kurt had always been tough. Farmers have to be. Once when Kurt was a kid in the sixth grade, he was helping his dad on the farm. He hopped off the tractor, but he wasn't careful about it and one of his feet landed right in the farm's corn picker. When working around farm equipment, you have to be really careful.

Bad accidents happen all the time. Kurt screamed as the corn picker mangled his foot. His dad rushed him to the hospital. It took several surgeries and lots of time in the hospital to recover. That was more than 50 years ago. He had learned his lesson. Or had he? All it takes to get in trouble around farm equipment is letting your guard down for just a second. One careless moment can kill you.

Kurt got out of bed before the sun came up, as usual. He had work to do, but it was work that he loved. The weather was perfect that day. It was April and the temperatures were warming up after the winter. Kurt needed to move a bunch of grain from his truck into the silo to store it. The grain goes into the hopper which separates it and then it gets pulled up a long chute or ramp. At the top it's dumped into the silo.

The hopper is attached to the tractor and the tractor turns it on. The hopper separates the kernels of grain with what is basically a heavy duty corkscrew that spins. It's really called an auger. The auger's spinning blades are what pulls the grain up the chute and into the silo. The auger has a protective covering over it so it doesn't hurt anyone. But that winter, Kurt had to cut a hole in the safety screen that covered the auger in order to fit it underneath his truck to catch the grain. He had meant to fix it.

As Kurt dumped the grain from the truck into the hopper, something went wrong. The grain was moving too quickly out of the truck and piling up everywhere. Kurt jumped into the hopper so that he could slow the grain going in. The grain had covered the hole Kurt had cut in the screen. Kurt was used to doing this and forgot about the hole. One of his feet went right through and into the blades of the auger.

As his foot went further than he expected, Kurt knew right away what was happening. The hole! It was too late. The auger had him. The spinning blades grabbed his leg and started pulling it down. His leg and his jeans were so entangled in the auger that he couldn't get them out, and the force of the auger was still pulling him down.

He desperately searched his pockets for his cell phone. It had actually fallen down into the grain and was lost. There was nobody around to hear him yell for help. Kurt was running out of options when suddenly, he remembered something. His pocket knife! Kurt had to do the unthinkable in order to save his own life. He had to cut off his own leg. Incredibly, the adrenaline of being in a life or death situation stifled the pain. He felt none. He just did what he had to do.

Once, he dropped the knife, but he was so focused that he caught it out of the air with his other hand. Kurt can't remember how long it all took. He only remembers falling out of the hopper. He was free, but there was still a lot to do to save his life.

He was around 200 feet away from his office where there was a phone. He had to crawl over gravel. Even though it was painful, he kept going without resting. He finally made it into the office and grabbed the phone. He called his son Adam, who was working at the fire station and told him he needed help.

Adam rushed to the farm and called 911. When he found his dad, he called the fire station and told them to get a helicopter ready. They didn't have much time. Kurt for his part, seemed pretty relaxed at this point. There was nothing left for him to do. Moments later he was in an ambulance and then the helicopter. Kurt looked down at the farmland below them for the entire helicopter ride.

His leg was now a stump but after a few months, he got a prosthetic leg and got back to work. When one of his farm workers went to visit Kurt in the hospital, Kurt immediately asked, "Why are you guys not working?" He was still a farmer first and foremost, and there's always work to do for a farmer. His workers joked that if they ever want to take a break, they'd have to steal Kurt's fake leg first.

Keys to Survival: This story is pretty extreme. I wouldn't have thought it even possible to just cut off your leg and crawl for help. When your life's on the line, some people dig deep and pull off the impossible. Kurt didn't panic. That's one of the keys here. He just got to work doing what he had to do. He knew that if he took any breaks crawling to the phone, he might pass out and not make it. So he just kept going. He's one tough farmer!

Rogue Grizzly Attacks 7 Teenagers

They were having the time of their lives. Their month in the National Outdoor Leadership School was wrapping up. The boys' parents had signed them up for an epic four week summer adventure. They would be learning all about how to survive in the wilderness of Alaska.

There were seven kids in total. Three boys were 16 years old, Noah, Shane, and Sam Boas. Three of the boys were 17, Josh, Sam and Sam Gottsegen, whose nickname was Gottsy. That left Victor who was the oldest at 18.

The month was almost over. They had learned first aid, survival skills, and had spent three glorious weeks backpacking with three instructors in Alaska's Talkeetna Mountains. This part of Alaska is beautiful, remote, and rugged. Their training was now over and the real test had begun. The instructors had left and it was up to the boys to hike 24 miles to a train track where they would meet back up with their instructors. They had three days to make the trip. No adults. Just seven kids alone in the wilderness. This was awesome and what they had been looking forward to all month. One of the instructors had joked as he left, "Don't Die!"

The boys had just caught a couple of trout in the creek. They would cook them up over that night's campfire. There were few trails here so they walked along the creek which was much easier than going through the thick forest. The creek twisted and turned. They couldn't see very far ahead. Josh was leading the way, as he often did. He rounded a bend in the creek and saw something. It was a brown mound in the middle of the creek. He was only 30 feet away. "Bear!" he screamed.

Josh had just let out that warning yell and the bear jumped on him in a flash. It was a giant grizzly. This bear was a lightning quick mountain of claws, fur, and teeth. Its roar shook the forest. It was on top of Josh before anyone could react.

The boys had been trained for this but in the moment of an actual bear attack, it's easy for all of that training to fly right out the window. A few of them had bear repellent. It didn't get used. The boys' instincts took over and they scattered out of the creek and up the embankment.

The bear still had Josh. His screams stopped Gottsy and Victor in their tracks. They whirled around and Victor, in terror, asked, "Is Josh being eaten?" Gottsy considered what he should do to save his friend, but the bear had already chosen him as its next target. Gottsy fought back but was no match for such a powerful predator. He was attacked just as brutally as Josh had been. Suddenly, all was quiet.

Noah was still down near Josh. He saw Shane up on the other side of the creek and silently mouthed "Where is it?" Shane had no idea either. Noah took his backpack off and rushed into the creek to help Josh. He didn't get there. The bear seemed to materialize out of thin air and slammed Noah with a mighty swipe of its claws. Then it bit into his chest and lifted him up into the air before dropping him. As Noah was lying there helpless, the bear stood up (seven feet tall) looking down at its victim. Was this it for Noah?

But instead, the bear caught sight of Shane, Boas, and Melman looking down at it from the embankment. This caused the bear to pause. It jumped over Noah and started to run away. As the bear began to retreat, he came across Victor. In one quick motion, he bit Victor in the leg. Victor managed to get in one good kick at the bear's head, which sent him scrambling into the woods. As quick as it had come, the bear disappeared over a small hill and was gone.

As it started to rain, Melman yelled to the others that their attacker was gone. Josh crawled toward his backpack. He was still alive! Noah met him, both boys were covered in blood. Josh told Noah to grab the emergency beacon. It was their only hope. Melman and Boas raced down the embankment to their wounded friends. Boas put Josh's head in his lap and commanded him not to move.

The boys dig out the beacon and quickly set it up and push the button. Now their location will be sent to a medical rescue team.

Meanwhile, Gottsy yelled for help. He made his way into an opening in the forest and collapsed. He has a hole in his chest. His lung has been punctured and he's in real trouble. Noah, despite his own injuries, quickly puts his recently learned first aid training to work. He fastened a wrap around Gottsy's chest that seals the wound, preventing air from going through it. It's emergency medicine at its finest, and prevents Gottsy's other lung from collapsing, which saves his life.

Josh is still being held by Boas and has what looks to be, the most dangerous injuries of the group. He was the first to be attacked and took the worst of it. His skull is fractured. He can't feel his legs. It's hard to tell where all of the blood is coming from. He no longer looks like himself because his head is so badly damaged.

Josh tells Melman to get his camera out of his backpack. He tells him to record a video. In it, with Boas cradling his head, Josh tells his parents and family goodbye. "I love you all, and I'm sorry I can't be with you." Josh is Jewish. When he's done with the video, he says the Jewish prayer, Shema Yisrael, which is sung when someone is dying as their final words.

Shane gets the tent set up. The boys carry Josh and Gottsy inside to get them dry and into sleeping bags. The boys use all their warm clothes to keep their injured friends warm. It's especially important to keep pressure on Gottsy's wound. They also need to keep Josh's head stabilized in case he has spine or neck injuries.

It continues to rain and the temperature falls. Everyone shivers and waits. At two in the morning, a helicopter finally lands near the tent. It's a state trooper. He takes one look at Josh and Gottsy and knows that he needs more medical help. Boas offers to stay with Josh and Gottsy, while the other boys are sent off in the helicopter.

The boys weep as they say goodbye. Noah, Victor, Melman, and Shane climb aboard the chopper and fly away. The state trooper, Boas, Josh, and Gottsy have to wait for another three hours. Finally, a huge National Guard helicopter sets down and medics rush inside the tent. Within minutes they're all airborne and hurtling toward a hospital. Their ordeal is nearly over.

Keys to Survival: There are hardly any instances of a grizzly bear attacking a group of more than four people. This was unique. This bear was hunted but never found. It may have been protecting a cub or a fresh kill. To avoid bear attacks, hike with a group and make noise as you go. Banging on a pot every so often should scare nearby bears away. You don't want to accidentally surprise one like these boys did. If you're attacked by a grizzly, your best bet is to go to the ground and play dead, holding your hands over your neck and head. You want to spread your legs out so that it can't flip you over. It's important to note that playing dead does not work against black bears. For those, you have to stand your ground and make lots of noise. If they still attack, then you have to fight by punching at their face. It's smart to know the difference between the two kinds of bears and what type you might encounter based on where you are.

The other key to saving Josh and Gottsy was the expert medical treatment that the boys did. With a punctured lung, you have to wrap it so that it's airtight in order to stabilize it or the other lung might also collapse. Gottsy would not have survived if both lungs had collapsed. The boys did their best to stop the bleeding and kept the boys as warm as they could. Thank goodness they were hiking with an emergency beacon. They all performed really bravely under pressure.

Running Out of Time in an Underwater Cave

When he wasn't teaching his students geology, you could usually find Xisco Grácia Lladòun cave diving. Actually, it's pretty hard to find a cave diver when they're in a cave so you probably wouldn't find him, now that I think about it. Xisco would experience exactly this situation with other divers trying to find him in a cave when he had to spend 60 hours stuck in the pitch darkness of a small cavern by himself, running out of air to breathe.

Xisco was an extremely experienced cave diver. He loved it almost as much as he loved his two children. It was his favorite pastime. He lives on the Mediterranean island, Majorca, which belongs to Spain. Majorca is a large island, 125 miles off the coast of mainland Spain. It has lots of underwater caves.

One fateful day in 2017, Xisco was getting ready for another adventure with his friend, Guillem Mascarò, who was also an experienced cave diver. The two men were excited to explore some unmapped underwater chambers that they knew were down there. They lowered themselves into the cold, dark water. They each had plenty of air in the scuba tanks. They even took an extra hour of air for each of them, just in case something went wrong.

Inside this underwater cave were ropes that divers used for finding their way around. The last thing you want to do while cave diving is get lost. The ropes were even numbered and had arrows pointing the way out. Seeing what number was on a rope told you exactly where you were inside the cave.

The two men followed the twists and turns for an hour before they reached their destination. They measured and explored the unmapped chamber. Another hour went by. Xisco took a look at the air gauge. They each had enough air for another two hours. With an hour trip ahead of them, this meant that it was time to go.

The way out of an underwater cave is usually more difficult than the way in. This is because a diver stirs up mud as they swim by. So as the diver heads back out, the water is no longer perfectly clear. It is muddier and harder to see. This is how most cave diving accidents happen. A diver gets lost in the muddy water. But Xisco and Guillem had the ropes to guide them...or so they thought.

As they started to move through the murky water, the rope they were following abruptly came to an end. Uh oh. The end of the rope was just lying there unattached to another rope. Xisco was able to communicate to Guillem that he should go wait in a nearby chamber with air. Some caves have small air spaces where air has been trapped. This gives the diver a chance to get some air to breathe without using their tank. Guillem could conserve the air in his tank while Xisco hunted for the next rope.

Xisco felt around everywhere for the next rope. This only stirred up more mud which made it even more difficult to see anything. He searched and searched. When he looked at his air gauge, he had used more than he thought. He realized with a sinking feeling that they each only had an hour left of air. He thought about how far they were from the cave exit. Even if they guessed correctly and found the way out, they wouldn't have enough time before running out of air. They were still more than a half mile inside the cave. Xisco went to find Guillem.

He came up out of the water and looked around. It was a big cavern. It was around 250 feet long and the ceiling of the chamber was 40 feet above the water. He told Guillem the bad news. He could also tell that there wasn't a whole lot of oxygen in this air. They started working on a plan.

Xisco pointed to another route out of the cave on his map. It was a longer swim but the rope should be good. Guillem looked at the air gauges and said, "There's only enough air for one of us to make it to the surface." Xisco replied, "You're smaller and quicker; you'll use less air on the way out." Xisco also felt that he had more experience breathing in air with higher levels of carbon dioxide like the air in this chamber.

Xisco watched Guillem swim away leaving him all alone in the dark cavern with no way out. This was not a good feeling. How long would it take until he gave in to carbon dioxide poisoning? Would Guillem even find his way out? He would have no way of knowing.

Guillem did get out and it only took him an hour to do it. He moved quickly to save his friend. Xisco would be slowly dying as he ran out of safe air to breathe. It only took another hour to get the rescue team to the cave entrance. These were the best divers in Majorca and they knew Guillem and Xisco well. It was starting to get dark outside.

Two divers who knew this cave went in first. Guillem showed them on the map exactly where Xisco was. Two hours passed and they were back out. The news was not good. The water was too muddy from Guillem getting out as fast as he could. The rescue divers couldn't read the signs on the ropes. Which way was Xisco? Ropes went down lots of different tunnels and if the rescue divers didn't know exactly where they were going, they might never be seen again. There was zero visibility in the cave, making rescue impossible. As hard as it was doing nothing, they knew that they would have to wait for the water to get clearer.

As word spread about the rescue effort, a big crowd gathered. The police came and took over the coordination of the rescue and reporters flocked to the scene. The head officer made the decision that no divers would enter the cave until morning to let the water clear. The divers couldn't believe it. Xisco might be dead by then!

Meanwhile, Xisco wasn't doing well. Alone in the darkness, his mind was racing with fear. He had no idea if anyone even knew that he was down there. His head hurt terribly from breathing in the bad air and he was dizzy. He couldn't sleep and was freezing. He even started to hear and see things that weren't there, like rescuers. Eventually his flashlight ran out of battery even though he wasn't using it much. All he could do was lie on the wet rock and think about his family.

Finally, the rescue divers were back in the water the next day. They were thrilled to find that the water was no longer muddy. They could see! One diver cut all the ropes except for the ones leading to Xisco. No one knew if Xisco was still alive but this step had to be done. Then another diver went to find Xisco, hoping that he was still breathing. When he eventually came out of the water into the big chamber, he yelled for Xisco. He was alive! The two men hugged.

Xisco asked, "Guillem is dead, isn't he?" "No, he's alive and waiting for you at the surface!" replied the rescuer, who was a friend of Xisco's. The diver gave Xisco a little food and determined that he was well enough to swim out. "I'm going back out to let them know you're alive. The next divers will bring you air and get you out of here. Can you wait a little longer?" Xisco excitedly responded with, "Now that I know I'm saved, I could wait another day!" He later said that, "It would take eight more hours to get me out of that cave, but they were eight happy hours."

It took another four hours for two of Xisco's diving buddies to get to him with tanks of air for him to use to swim out. He greedily breathed his first big breath of good air in nearly 60 hours. He immediately started to feel better. When he came out of the cave, the big crowd went crazy. They had done it. Xisco was alive after 60 hours in the sea cave. Guillem was there to give him a big hug before the ambulance took him to the hospital.

Keys to Survival: Even though Xisco and Guillem had plenty of experience and were good cave divers, life threatening situations can still happen. They made the right decision for one of them to go get help. They would have drowned if they had both tried to escape. Xisco really had to trust Guillem, but Guillem didn't let him down! The rescue effort came together quickly even though they had to wait for the water to clear. That was the right decision also. Rescue cave divers have died by going into muddy water too early and getting lost. By being safe, everyone ended up surviving. Also, Xisco had to remain calm and not give up down there. That was extremely hard to do, as I'm sure that you can imagine! Thoughts of his family kept him fighting for life as long as he could.

Quicksand!

Quicksand is a terrible name for this dangerous trap. Quicksand could not be any slower about killing someone. It's like getting stuck in concrete. You just sit there. Don't be fooled, quicksand can be deadly. This is the story of a nature photographer who nearly died in it.

Ryan Osmun was hiking with his girlfriend in Zion National Park in Utah. This is an extremely popular park and it's huge. The park is 229 square miles and there are more than 100 great trails to choose from. Ryan was out there in February when there weren't as many other hikers.

Ryan and his girlfriend, Jessika, had chosen a 9-mile hike. Around mid-day, they were halfway along the trail and it had just started to snow lightly. It was a canyon trail with steep sides rising up on either side. There was a little pond in their way with no way around it. It didn't look deep, so they headed through it. Jessika was almost to the other side when one foot sank into sand and then the other. She was sinking. Ryan was behind her and quickly grabbed her and pushed her up and out. Jessika was able to get to the other side of the quicksand.

But now Ryan couldn't follow her. He was stuck. The quicksand went all the way up to his thigh of one leg and up over his other foot as well. He managed to get his left foot free. It was the one that wasn't as buried as his right leg. His right leg was going nowhere. It was like being stuck in concrete. The good thing was that he wasn't sinking further, but he was trapped.

There was no cell phone service on this trail. Luckily, Ryan wasn't hiking alone. He would not have survived. They decided that Jessika would go back for help. The two of them weren't having any luck at all in freeing Ryan. Jessika handed him a stick to use to push himself out but it was no use. She would have to get help on her own, so she set off.

Jessika had only been gone for a half-hour before it started to snow. Fortunately, Ryan had a warm jacket on and zipped the hood tight around his face and head. Then Ryan came the closest he would get to dying in the quicksand. He fell asleep. He woke up with a start as he was falling back into the quicksand. That was a close one! He knew that if the top part of his body went in, he might not get out at all.

The sun was setting and darkness fell. Ryan had been alone for five hours. It started to get much colder. To make matters worse, Ryan was completely soaked with both sweat and the water on top of the quicksand. He was thinking that he might not survive the night. At one point he got his hopes up when he thought he saw a flashlight, but it was only the moon.

So when he saw another light an hour later, he thought his mind might be playing tricks on him but he yelled anyway. This time it was help! Jessika had made it. It was a man named Tim who had more help coming behind him. They had to wait another hour, but finally, Tim's companions made it to where Ryan was stuck. They would use a pulley system to rescue him.

They tied ropes to a large boulder that was nearby. They tied the other end of the rope to Ryan's leg that was so deep in the quicksand. Two of the men held Ryan's arms while they pulled on the rope. It took a while because the quicksand had such a firm grip on Ryan's leg.

Finally, Tim could grab an ankle. They were getting close. And after a few more pulls with the ratchet, Ryan was finally free after sitting there for 12 hours. But he was unable to walk. His leg was swollen and he had no feeling in it at all.

A helicopter would not work in all the darkness and the swirling snow so they had to wait until morning to get to a hospital. The rescuers were prepared for this. They had brought sleeping bags and gave Ryan some medicine for the pain. When he woke up the next day, he was covered in snow. It kept snowing until lunchtime. Finally, a helicopter could get to them and they airlifted Ryan to the hospital.

His leg was huge and swollen. But x-rays showed that there were no broken bones.

Ryan was just glad to be in a warm bed and out of the quicksand and off of that trail. Ryan didn't think he would live through that night, but he hung in there. Thanks to Jessika and the work of the experienced rescue team, he was safe.

Keys to Survival: Ryan never panicked despite being worried as his ordeal went on and on. Quicksand is usually not very deep. But the more you move, the more stuck you get. Jessika gave Ryan a long stick that helped. By holding it flat on the ground, it spread out the weight and kept him from falling in further. This stick could have also helped if coyotes or some other predator had found him. Ryan also had plenty of water. The main thing was that Ryan wasn't alone. He had someone to go get help. That is what saved his life.

Merle, the Miracle Dog

Dogs are awesome. Nearly everyone loves dogs. They're cute, protective, and wonderful companions. This is the story of one dog who got in trouble, but somehow survived the impossible.

Merle was an Australian Shepherd and his owners had only had him for a few months. He was just a year old and loved to go running with his new best friend and owner, Eric Wagenknecht. Eric had been excited when he learned that his new puppy loved to run as much as he did.

Eric and Merle went on long runs all the time. Today, Eric took Merle to a trail in the Colorado mountains. It was a good climb, eight miles up to the top of Grand Traverse Peak, and then eight miles back. But this would be no problem for Merle.

It was a beautiful morning in the early Summer and the air was crisp. The pair of runners were near the top of the mountain and feeling great. They had almost made it. In the moment that Eric's feet landed on the very top of the mountain, he heard Merle let out a quick yelp behind him.

When Merle didn't join him at the top, Eric looked around. What was Merle doing? Merle was such a fit and capable dog, that it didn't occur to Eric that he might be in trouble. But as he looked for his dog, it was as if Merle had disappeared. Then he saw something. Eric let out a gasp.

Hundreds of feet down the side of the mountain, he saw paw prints in a patch of snow. They vanished off the side. Below that ledge with the snowy paw prints was a steep slope about 800 feet long. At the bottom of that slope was a deadly looking cliff. Eric immediately knew that Merle's yelp was a cry for help as he slipped off the mountain.

Eric frantically looked everywhere for signs of Merle. There was no way that he could get down to that ledge without a rope and climbing equipment. Merle's path down the mountain looked nearly straight down. Then Eric's heart filled with joy. There was Merle! He seemed to be running down below the cliff. He was way down there. Eric was going to get to him, somehow.

He went back down the trail as quickly as he could. Eventually, he made his way down to where he had seen Merle from the top of the mountain. And there he was! Merle was still there, but when Eric called to him, Merle ran in the other direction. He was really scared.

Eric could see that Merle was in pretty bad shape. He was covered in cuts, swollen, and not moving very well. Just as Eric got near him, Merle jumped down into a tiny little cave in the snow and rocks. Eric managed to grab his back leg but couldn't hang on. Nothing he said or did could coax Merle out. He stayed there for an hour. Then the sound of Merle's breathing and the clinking of his collar finally went silent. There was no sound at all from the darkness of the tiny cave.

Eric was miserable. This was all his fault. Merle was such a loving, happy little dog who had trusted him completely. He would have to go home and tell his family that their dog had died. What had started as such a fun and wonderful day, had taken a sad turn. He had left an open can of sardines by the mouth of the cave when he was trying to get Merle to come out. He didn't bother to get it. Eric made the lonely trip home.

Eric still felt awful. His vet told him that it was normal for a dog to behave the way Merle had when it's injured. If they're about to die, they prefer to find a hidden place all by themselves. This didn't make Eric feel much better about things. But he had waited as long as he could by the cave. It wouldn't have been safe to try to hike back after dark.

More than 20 days later, a realtor was at a house that she was getting ready to sell. Her name was Dana Gumber. The house was close to where Eric had parked the car for his run with Merle three weeks earlier. Dana saw a limping, mangy little dog in the yard. When she came back a couple hours later, the dog was lying on the front doormat!

She could see it closer now and knew that it needed help. It was really thin. She knew it must be hungry. It was really dirty, too but it seemed like a nice dog and it had a collar. Dana had a big heart for dogs. She took this poor little guy home and got him some water and food. She also saw the dog's name on his collar and there was a phone number. So she called Eric's number and left a message that she had his dog.

Eric had flown to Europe for work when he got the voicemail message from Dana. Could this be right? Was it a prank? Eric called his wife Susan and she said she would call the lady back to find out what was going on. When she heard that Merle was still alive, she could hardly believe it.

Susan went to Dana's house and Merle seemed grateful to see her but something wasn't quite right with him. She took him right to the animal hospital. The veterinarian told Susan that Merle didn't have any broken bones which was amazing. But Merle had lost a lot of weight. He had survived by eating berries and leaves. One of his lungs was punctured in the fall and both of his retinas were detached. That's why he hadn't seemed quite right to Susan. His eyes couldn't focus. The retina is in the eye and if Merle's stayed detached for much longer, he could go blind. He needed a lot of care!

Merle had fallen down a mountain, and then a 40-foot cliff. He walked 20 miles to the house where Dana had found him and helped him. The family veterinarian thought that he must have gone into a coma in the cave which is why it sounded to Eric like his breathing stopped. When Merle woke up, he must have found the sardines that Eric had left behind. The vet said that it's very rare for a dog to live that long in the wild.

Merle made a full recovery. When Eric got home from his trip, he wasn't sure what to expect. Would Merle still act mad at him? But Merle eagerly hopped into his lap and was happy to be reunited with his running partner again. That is one tough dog!

Keys to Survival: Merle was one determined dog. It's really remarkable that he survived the fall alone, much less the three weeks to get back to civilization! He ate pine needles because he was so hungry, and he found some berries, too. We know that because the vet saw them in his poop. Somehow he avoided bears and mountain lions on his hike back. Dogs have really great senses of smell. So Merle must have used his nose to follow the trail and that's how he found people as well. He had to rely on smell because his vision wasn't very good with his retinas detached. That can happen in a fall if your head is hit hard. He also must have really loved his family to keep going as hurt as he was.

"I'm Going In!"
A Terrifying Shark Story

The waves that had crashed so violently all night had calmed down. The water was freezing and he was cramping up. He'd been swimming all night. There was a trail of blood behind him from the wound on his forehead where it hit the instrument panel of the plane as he crashed into the ocean. He also had a gash on his leg. Rescuers wouldn't have much of a chance at spotting him. The plane was deep beneath the sea by now, but his blood was probably working as an emergency beacon to any shark within a mile or two of where he was. Not great. Then he felt the unmistakable bump of something big under his feet. They'd found him.

Walter Wyatt, Jr. was now 37 years old, after serving as a fighter pilot in the Vietnam War when he was younger. Living in Florida, he had just spent a fun weekend in the Bahamas. It was December 1986, and time to fly back home. During his stay, some thieves had stolen his plane's navigational equipment. That was annoying, but Walter was an experienced pilot. He was flying a Beechcraft twin engine plane with just a compass and a battery powered radio. That's definitely a risky way to fly! But at least he wasn't getting shot at, flying in a war zone. The weather was good. This would be a piece of cake compared to flying in Vietnam.

The flight was just an hour from the Bahamas to Miami. He should be able to see the lights of Miami for most of the flight. Unfortunately, the weather took an unexpected turn for the worse. His compass started acting crazy, too. Was he off course? The clouds got dark and the heavy rain hit. He couldn't see much but he could make out some rocks down below. Maybe that was Bimini? It wasn't. He was lost.

He sent out a mayday call on his radio and got through to the Coast Guard out of Miami. It took an hour for the rescue jet to find him. It was a reassuring sight for Walter to have that in the sky along beside him. The pilot was Lieutenant Steven Blankenship. "We'll get you down, buddy." Lt. Steven led Walter in the direction of an emergency runway on Cay Sal.

Cay Sal is a tiny island chain right in the middle of Cuba, Key West, and the Bahamas. Walter WAS off course. He wasn't supposed to be down there. Walter was running low on fuel and could hear one of his two engines faltering. Lt. Steven radioed, "Hang in there, Walter, six miles and you'll be there." He wouldn't make it.

Even though he still had a quarter tank of gas for his left engine, it wasn't making it through the line. Then the right engine cut out. His left engine ran dry, too. Walter was only going in one direction now. Down.

As his small plane started to nose dive, he radioed, "I'm going in!" Lt. Steven could only watch in horror as Walter's plane disappeared into the ocean. He made several passes over where he saw the plane's lights disappear but couldn't see anything. He and his co pilot had no choice but to head back for Key West to refuel. They thought that Walter must not have survived, but they would come back when they got more fuel.

Walter was very much alive, standing on the wing of his plane, trying to get some signal flares lit. The Coast Guard plane flew right over him. The flares had gotten wet and just fell apart with a spark that only sputtered. His plane sank quickly and Walter was now drifting in the angry ocean. Fortunately, he had grabbed a life vest, but it was only working on one side. Still, that was enough, but how would anyone find him now?

He started swimming in the direction that Sal Cay must be. But in the big waves of the storm, it didn't take long to get turned around. He had no idea what direction the land was. He was cold, really cold. He had been in the water for two hours now and it was nearly 10:00 at night. There was only darkness all around him. There was darkness below him, too. He felt something big bump into his legs. It could only be one thing.

He had been bleeding for the past two hours. There was no helping that. He had a deep cut on his leg and one on his forehead. He knew that it was only a matter of time before sharks found him. How in the world was he going to make it through this?

The Coast Guard jet had refueled and was back out searching for him. It led a helicopter to where Walter's plane went down. The helicopter had a spotlight and would try to find the floating man in the stormy sea. That's not an easy task, especially during a storm. The rain only got stronger and the storm raged. Both the jet and the helicopter had to go back and wait until morning.

Walter was glad to have the rain water falling into his open mouth. But then he felt another shark bump into his legs. He kicked it as hard as he could. He wouldn't be eaten without a fight!

That last shark bump was at midnight. Walter was thrilled to see the sun peeking up over the horizon. He had made it to morning! As the sun started to light up his surroundings, he could actually see the danger that was circling him. There were shark fins poking out of the water, *everywhere*.

One came right at him and bumped his arm as it swam by. The storm had passed and he was no longer bobbing up and down in the waves. That was good for sea sickness, but now the sharks didn't have the waves to slow them down. The calm water would only make it easier for them to catch their prey.

Walter was spinning all around, not wanting to miss one coming for his back. A hefty bull shark made a charge and then dove. He looked down to see it coming up at him from below with its jaws open. He placed a well timed kick right on its face. The shark shot away from him and then resumed circling. More bull sharks made charges. Big hammerhead sharks were there, too and seemed even quicker.

Then he saw another killer join the pack. A giant mako shark crested the water. Walter knew that makos were the fastest predator in the ocean, and this was a big one. It poked its head up out of the water close to Walter, too close. It looked him right in the eye, before disappearing. He would later say, "I was freaked, I tell you - that was like the devil looking into my own eyes." Walter did his best not to panic. Once one shark bit him, he knew that they would all be on him. Then it would be over.

At that moment, he heard it. Lieutenant Steven and the Coast Guard jet were back! It was so close, c'mon! The jet was flying in a search pattern and miraculously passed right over Walter who was waving his orange life jacket trying to catch his attention.

Lt. Steven was looking for the plane wreckage. He didn't think there was any possibility of a survivor. But...was that? No way. That's him! Incredibly, in all that open ocean. Lt. Steven was looking down at a single man waving a life jacket. He got on the radio with a Coast Guard ship that was in the area. "Hey, there's a guy in the water!" The Coast Guard ship was a cutter, called the Cape York. It was only twelve minutes away. Would that be fast enough?

Lt. Steven dropped a smoke signal down to Walter so that the cutter could see the smoke and go right for him. He could actually see Walter swimming for the canister that was spitting out the smoke. Then chills went down his spine because he saw something else, too. There was an enormous shadow under the water following Walter.

"Get moving, cutter! There's a shark targeting this guy!" Lt. Steven had already lost Walter once. He didn't want to find him after fifteen hours only to watch him get eaten by a giant shark.

Walter kept spinning around and glancing underneath him as he waited. Please God, please. Minutes passed and he saw it, the most beautiful thing he had ever seen. It was a shiny Coast Guard cutter racing toward him.

It pulled up and Walter saw a rope ladder thrown down at him, but he couldn't climb anything after floating and fighting sharks for 15 hours in the cold sea. He had no strength left at all. Two servicemen climbed down to pull him to safety. He fell onto the deck and kissed it. He couldn't believe he was still alive. Lt. Steven saw it all unfold from above and pumped his fist.

He couldn't believe it either! Who was this guy?

After being released from the hospital, Walter drifted into sleep saying, "I can't believe I'm alive!" He never did let go of his orange life jacket. He still has it to this day.

Keys to Survival: This might be the scariest survival story in this book. Lots of things saved Walter's life in this story. Radioing the Coast Guard was one. Grabbing the life jacket was another. Walter credited God as well. He said, "If you don't believe in God, you do when you hit the water. So you pray. And you pray, and you pray, and you pray." Walter was also full of fight. Having the mental strength to fight off sharks as long as he did showed amazing stamina. Punch and kick at the shark's eyes and nose with all your might and sometimes that's enough to convince them to go find an easier meal.

Attacked by an Arctic Predator

It was 3:30 in the morning when Rich bolted awake in his tent. Screams pierced the cold air all around him. Something was terribly wrong. As he scrambled out of his tent, the massive polar bear was already running away. But it had something. Was that the body of one of his friends? His heart filled with dread. The bear had the person's head in its jaws!

Rich Gross and Marta Chase loved what they did. They led hiking trips for the Sierra Club. The Sierra Club is an advocacy group for the environment, dedicated to protecting the earth's wilderness areas. They also offer cool expeditions that people can join.

Rich thought that a trip to northern Canada's Torngat Mountains National Park would be really exciting. It's one of the least visited National Parks and it was appealing to go somewhere that few people had ever been. Rich had never seen a wild polar bear. That would be amazing. Marta was a bit more nervous about being around wild polar bears. That can be incredibly dangerous and demands a lot of careful planning.

Polar bears aren't like other bears. If they see a person, they are much more likely to hunt them. They aren't as fearful of humans as other bears are. Polar bears are very sneaky hunters. They eat fish, but really love seals. They wait above the seals' breathing holes in the ice. When an unlucky seal pops their head out to breathe, the polar bear bites down on their head. Lunch.

Polar bears eat more meat than other bears. Of course, there's just not as many berries or plants in the Arctic Circle where they live. They're also bigger than other kinds of bears. They can stand up to 10 feet tall and weigh more than 1,500 pounds. They are powerful and can be deadly for people. Fortunately, they don't come into contact with many people where they live. That is, until people come looking for them.

Rich and Marta had five people joining them on this adventure. Their companions were Larry, Marilyn, Rick, Matt, and Marta's husband, Kicab. A sea plane dropped the group off. The surroundings were wildly beautiful and very few people had ever seen it.

The Labrador Sea separates Canada from Greenland before it empties into the Atlantic. The seven adventurers were not far from the coast. They were staying just off the shore of the Nachvak Fjord. A land of snow covered mountains, icy lakes, and waterfalls surrounded them.

Groups like this will often hire local bear guards who are trained in how to deal with the bears. These guards are usually Inuit, the native people of this region, and allowed to carry guns for protection. But Rich and Marta were talked out of that by a local outfitter. They were told that all they needed was an electric fence around their camp, bear spray, and flares. So that's what they did. They set up one fence around their camp and another around their food preparation area.

The fences came up to Rich's waist and had three strands of wire. They would not stun or kill a bear, only zap it enough to give it a good scare. The group had a nice meal and went to sleep. Kicab was up early that morning and soon everyone else would be, too. "Polar bear on the beach!"

This was what everyone had been looking forward to. They climbed out of their tents and were treated to an adorable sight. A mom and her baby cub were calmly walking along the water. Wild polar bears! This scene filled the hearts of the group. This was such a special thing to see. The momma bear had no interest in bothering the people and she walked on by with her cub. It was precious.

Later that morning, the hiking would begin. They were ready to explore, and they did exactly that. They hiked all day. Heading back to camp that afternoon, they encountered a curious onlooker. There was a big male polar bear walking right at them. He was hundreds of yards away but when he saw them, he headed their way.

The group did what they were trained to do. They got together and stood tall. They made lots of noise and yelled at the bear. But still it came. He was bigger than the mama bear from that morning. Finally, it was too close for comfort. At just 50 yards away, Rich fired his flare gun. The flare blasted out and made a lot of noise. The bear did not stop. It kept right on coming. The flare fell out of the sky and landed right by the bear. Finally, that made it run off.

Relief flooded the group of hikers. Thank goodness! They laughed and cheered. But the polar bear didn't run far. It stopped a few hundred feet away and laid down, keeping an eye on them. It could see their camp, too, from its new perch.

It started to rain. The group had been up early and hiked far that day. It was a great time for a nap. Matt didn't feel great being watched by this bear that didn't seem scared of them. He watched it right back for the next hour, both of them sitting in the rain. Eventually Matt's fatigue won out and he went inside his tent for some rest.

Later that evening, the group laughed and ate. Still, the bear stayed at a distance, watching. Most of the group weren't too worried about it. But Matt couldn't shake that uneasy feeling and asked Rich if they should stay up in shifts to keep watch. Rich tried to make Matt feel better about it and told him that the electric fence would keep them safe. Get some rest.

Rick shared Matt's concern. He didn't sleep well being watched by a polar bear, so he kept checking on it through the night. It was always just sitting there but sometime after midnight, it was gone. Okay, that's good. Maybe he was worried for nothing.

The next morning, there was no bear. Phew! The group had another great day hiking. They saw whales and had a ton of fun. This place was special. Everyone turned in for the night after dinner. They were tired and happy. Rich checked the fence, it was on. He crawled into his sleeping bag with his flare gun close by.

That night, it happened. It was 3:30 and Rich woke up to screaming. Marta was yelling his name. She happened to wake up and look out her tent window. She found herself looking right into the face of the polar bear. Its face was only feet from hers! It started dragging one of the other tents away into the night.

Rich shot out of his tent as quickly as he could. The bear was getting away. It was about 25 yards away from him and moving fast. But it had what it came for. Rich was shocked to see the body of Matt being dragged by the bear. They were going to the water. Others were up and yelling now. Rich fired the flare and handed the gun to Marta. Rick joined him and the two ran toward the bear.

More than 200 feet from the camp, they found Matt where the bear had dropped him.

They hadn't expected him to be alive but Rick saw that he was breathing. Fortunately, Rick had been a doctor before he retired. He got right to work.

The group protected Matt from the weather and covered him with blankets. Matt had been awake the entire time he had been dragged by the bear. He had woken up and seen the two huge paws tear at his tent. He screamed and then the bear bit down on his head and began to move. He said that the bear's breath stank like fish. He was surprised that he stayed so calm. He quickly accepted that he was about to die. In the shock of what was happening, he didn't hurt.

But he was definitely hurt. When a polar bites down on your head and drags you 200 feet, you're really lucky to stay alive. Matt had several head wounds, but the scariest wound was Matt's neck. Rick could actually see his main artery through a hole in his neck. That artery is what carries most of your blood to your heart. Matt would die in less than a minute if it tore. It was a miracle that it was still intact.

This was a terrifying situation. For one, that bear was still out there in the dark. And two, Rick had no idea how long it would take to get Matt to a hospital. They were hundreds of miles out in the wilderness. Their first aid supplies weren't exactly meant to fix an injury as bad as this. Rick felt that Matt's best chance was prayer.

The group was relieved when the sun finally came up. Now at least they weren't in as much danger of a sneak attack. Rich had called in their emergency on the satellite phone as soon as they got Matt back into camp. A rescue helicopter landed at 8:30. It had been more than four hours and Matt was still hanging on.

Matt's journey to a hospital that was equipped to deal with the extent of his injuries would take a long time. It would end up being 20 hours since being in the mouth of the polar bear when he was finally wheeled into a room at the Montreal hospital.

Matt's jaw was broken. He had a collapsed lung, a broken hand, and two of the vertebrae in his spine were broken. All this was from an attack that lasted a few seconds. He was covered in wounds and he still has scars on his face, but he survived! Before the trip he had several tattoos of animals on his body. He got a new one of a polar bear with six stars around it, one star for each of his friends who did what they could to save him.

Matt has even been back to the campsite that he was attacked at. He went back with both Rich and Marta, but this time they had a couple of Inuit guards with real guns. He saw some polar bears, but didn't recognize any of them as his attacker. Luckily, this time none of the bears got close enough for anyone to smell their fish breath or face any danger.

Keys to Survival: If the polar bear had gotten to the water, Matt would have drowned and been that bear's breakfast. He's also incredibly lucky that the bear's tooth that went into his neck didn't reach his artery. There were extra precautions that could have been made to avoid the attack, but at least Rich had a satellite phone to get help. He also bravely charged into the darkness to save Matt. They were lucky that the bear dropped him when the flare was shot.

That flare saved his life. Polar bears are very scary creatures and powerful hunters. It's best to be armed with more than flares if you're in their territory.

Go Downhill and Follow Water

This wasn't looking good. The fog was everywhere. They couldn't see anything. They were in a small plane in the mountains. Nope, this wasn't good at all.

Autumn Veach was 16 years old. The plan had been for her family to drive her back from Montana to her home in northern Washington, but her step-grandparents offered to fly her. That sounded much more fun and it would be much faster. Autumn's step-grandparents were experienced pilots. But when you're surrounded by fog AND your GPS goes out? It doesn't matter how experienced you are.

They were in the Cascades mountain range in Washington after flying for an hour and a half. That's when the trouble started. They flew into a whiteout. Autumn's step-grandad just barely avoided a mountain after it suddenly loomed into view through the fog. That was a close one. Would their luck continue? It wouldn't. They crashed. Autumn jumped out of the back seat on the driver's side and tried to pull her step-grandad out of the plane. But he was dazed and still buckled in. The fire was swallowing everything and burned Autumn badly on the hand. She couldn't help. She tried and tried but it was already too late.

She was crying and running. The plane exploded right behind her. She was running wildly downhill and went over a small cliff edge and landed hard. She knew she had to calm down, but she was by herself in a mountain wilderness after an extremely traumatic experience. Now she was hurt. She lay there for several moments thinking back to the survival shows she had seen on television. Some very good advice from those shows suddenly came to her. Go downhill. Follow water.

Autumn thought she heard an interstate. It was a river which wasn't as good but still helpful. She started to walk. It can be really hard to follow a river downhill through the wilderness. Autumn kept having to cross the river when she couldn't keep going on one side because of cliffs and boulders. This difficult hike had her soaking wet. The night started to fall and Autumn was a mess. She was sobbing for her step-grandparents. She was scared and cold and not at all sure that she would live through this.

She took off the clothes that were the most soaked and wrapped up in her cardigan. She laid down in the driest spot she could find. She still felt a lot of pain from her burns so there wasn't much sleeping, but she made it through the night. It was a very long and extremely uncomfortable night, but she survived. The hunger, the pain, and the fatigue were getting to her.

She set out as soon as it started to get light. After an hour of more difficult trekking, she was ready to give up. She felt terrible in every way. Everything hurt. That's when she got angry. She thought about how unfair it was that she was going to die. This motivated her to keep going. She kept pushing through the forest for the rest of the day. She saw a search plane at one point, but they couldn't hear her screams.

Autumn started praying as she trudged along. She was desperate and depressed. The night was coming again. She laid down by the river but tonight sleep would be even harder. Mosquitos and sand fleas were tormenting her. It was impossible to be comfortable. But again, she made it through another terrible night by the river.

When she got up in the morning, she felt like today had to be the day. She had been hiking for two days. Surely she had to be close to finding someone at this point. This gave Autumn the hope she needed. After following the river, on her 3rd day she saw what looked like a small wooden bridge. Maybe it wasn't really there. It couldn't be. But as she got closer and stepped onto it, her heart leaped. This was a sign that she was getting close.

Beyond the bridge was an even better sign. It was a parking lot. And even better, a road! Autumn looked terrible but she walked to the side of the road to flag down some help. Thankfully the road was not deserted. There were cars, but nobody would stop! They just kept driving past her despite all her frantic waving. This went on for a whole hour before she gave up. There was one car in the parking lot. Eventually, they would come back and they would have to help her. She sat down and waited. Finally, another car pulled in. Autumn, exhausted, began to cry. The people gave her Gatorade and drove her to the closest town where she called 911.

She had done it. Autumn would be okay.

Keys to Survival: It wasn't easy and Autumn had nothing to help her survive except the clothes she was wearing. But fortunately, she remembered two very important rules for escaping the wilderness. Go downhill. Follow water. Water usually leads to more water...and people. Going downhill saves your energy and the water will keep you from dying from dehydration. You don't want to overdo it with unpurified or untreated water because you can get sick. But you'll need it to survive long enough to find people to help you. You can't live for more than 3 days without water. If you can't find any water to follow, walking downhill will often lead you eventually to water because water travels downhill, too.

Inches Away From Drowning

Roderick turned to his friend and said, "If we don't make it, I want you to know I love you, brother." Brandon grinned and responded, "Shut up, bro, you know I love you, too."

Roderick and Brandon were both in the Air Force and stationed at the Kadena Air Base in Japan. They both had a shift as guards at the ammunition storage depot on the base. It would be very dangerous if anyone broke in there. There was a guard shack at the entrance where the two airmen controlled who went in and out.

For the past couple of days, Japan had been getting hit by a really serious typhoon. (A typhoon is the same thing as a hurricane, but in Japan, they're called typhoons.) The winds had gotten all the way up to 100 miles per hour! Thankfully, the storm had calmed down.

The wind had been replaced by a persistent rain. There seemed to be no relief from the rain. It just kept coming. Roderick and Brandon had the night shift guarding the ammunition depot. They got there at 10 pm. As the two friends walked to the guard shack, Brandon saw a giant puddle a few hundred yards away and said with a chuckle, "Bro, I bet that water's going to be up to the shack by morning." Roderick didn't argue Brandon's point, he just hoped that they could go back to their bunks before they had to worry about it.

There weren't many trucks going through the gate that night in the storm, so the two airmen got a lot of studying done. They were going through a career advancement course and had work to do. When the sun came up, it was still pouring. Everything looked soaked. Fortunately, Roderick and Brandon had stayed nice and dry in the guard shack.

Brandon was watching the weather out the window and laughed. "See? I told you." The big puddle had nearly reached the guard shack door. What a mess! After another hour, both guys jumped at a crashing noise. Looking out, they both saw that the giant puddle was now a fast moving river. There was lots of junk in it moving quickly through the parking lot. This was starting to get a little more serious.

Brandon tried to open the door. It was stuck. They hadn't realized that the water had risen so much. There was too much water against the door to push it open. Brandon told Roderick, "You try, you're bigger." Roderick slammed his shoulder into the door. It still didn't budge. This WAS serious!

He got on the radio with the base operations center. He told them, "We're in trouble. We're going to need somebody to come and get us." Roderick was told that the flooding wasn't just his guard shack, but all over the base. It would be a bit before any patrols arrived to help. Still, the operator radioed in Roderick's distress call and waited.

The water was rising faster and was now actually inside the guard shack. It was up over their boots.

But outside? It was now higher than the bottom of the window. Roderick and Brandon were getting more than they had bargained for and hoped that the shack would hold up to suddenly being in a river.

They cut off the electricity so they wouldn't risk being electrocuted. They climbed up out of the water. But the water kept rising quickly. The two friends felt good seeing the fire truck get there, but by then the water was *above* the window. They could actually see fish swimming by. This morning kept getting weirder by the minute!

The operator who had taken Roderick's distress call was T. Sgt. Kevin Spain. He didn't like the sound of Roderick and Brandon's situation. As soon as he could, he headed to them. When Kevin saw the guard shack, he became extremely worried for the two guards. The shack was down the hill from the gate and already nearly underwater! They had to move fast. The two guards were in danger of drowning, and soon!

Roderick and Brandon only had a couple feet of air left in the shack. Roderick tried to shoot out the window with his gun. Unfortunately, the guard shack windows were bulletproof. He shot it 15 times and didn't even crack it. The two guards were completely helpless. All they could do was tell jokes to stay calm.

Soon enough, there were eight rescuers standing on top of the guard shack, all banging on it with sledge hammers and axes. The concrete roof was a foot thick. It had been made to withstand a grenade attack. The rescuers were getting nowhere.

Roderick and Brandon could hear the banging. They just had inches of breathing room and were treading water to keep their mouths in the air. They both started to pray. They might actually die in this stupid thing! Brandon's only thought was, "Please don't do this to my mom."

Roderick's head bumped the ceiling and it gave a little. So he started pushing on it and was able to pull it down which gave the two desperate men another two feet of air. Hallelujah!

Then, another fire truck arrived with a concrete saw. Maybe the rescuers would get somewhere with that. Roderick and Brandon heard the saw fire up above them and hit the concrete. They cheered and pounded the ceiling as they saw two long slits appear. But then there was nothing. What was happening, why did they stop?

The saw had jammed. Good grief, there's no time for this! The rescuers went back to their sledge hammers with a determined ferocity. They HAD to get through. Concrete was falling down on the faces of Roderick and Brandon. They didn't mind. Please, please, please!

But once the concrete was broken through, the men groaned when they saw thick steel rods remaining. This was heavy duty rebar, and you couldn't just bang your way through it. They could see and talk to Roderick and Brandon now, but it looked like they had come this far only to watch them drown. There were only inches of air left and their fellow servicemen were still stuck in an underwater cage.

The rescuers used a bolt cutter to get a little ways through the steel bars and then an ax to finish the cut. It was grueling and slow. Finally, there was an opening.

Roderick watched as Brandon was pulled out. Then the hands came for Roderick. But his shoulders were too wide for the hole. He wouldn't fit. Now the rescuers went berserk in their panic to save Roderick. At least now he could stick his entire head out of the hole to get a breath before he went under so that the men above could hammer away at the steel.

Brandon refused to go to the ambulance that had pulled up. "I'm not leaving until my wingman does!" The hole got a bit wider. They tried again. This time, the broad shouldered cadet fit through the hole. The exhausted rescuers yelled and hugged each other. It had been an hour since Roderick had called for help. As he stood on the roof of the guard shack for the first time, the rain suddenly stopped. The men doubled over with laughter at the ridiculousness of the timing.

There were 17 rescuers who were given Air Force medals for their heroism during that flood. Roderick said, "They were there for us all the way. They were willing to do whatever it took to get us out."

The new guard shack was built with an escape hatch.

Keys to Survival: As soon as you know you're in trouble, it is crucial to call for help. This is true of any survival situation and true on that day at the Kadena Air Base. Sometimes you don't really know that you're in a survival situation until it gets really bad. If Roderick hadn't called for help as soon as they discovered they were stuck, they wouldn't have made it.

The 7th Grader Who
Had to Save His Dad

Alaska is the biggest wilderness area in the United States. And the second biggest? It's the Frank Church River of No Return Wilderness in Idaho. It's *2.3 million* acres. That's big! And that's where Charlie Finlayson was hiking with his dad, David. Charlie was 13 and he and his dad had gone on lots of adventures together.

David was a mountain climber. He loved being outdoors. He loved doing it with his son, Charlie. Charlie had learned a lot about climbing with ropes and he was ready for this. They'd be gone for two weeks. They spent two days hiking to their campsite. It was next to a mountain lake, surrounded by fun mountains to climb.

They were having a blast. The weather was great and Charlie couldn't believe how beautiful and exciting everything was. There they were, climbing one of the mountain peaks, 800 feet up. David was in a harness with Charlie holding the rope in case he fell. Charlie was tied to a tree. The two were safe climbers.

David was climbing on the wall of the mountain when he heard something really loud. A boulder the size of a refrigerator had come loose and fell away from the mountain. It smashed into David as it fell. Charlie could no longer see his Dad but felt the rope catch him. He yelled for him but his dad didn't answer. It must have seemed like a lifetime to Charlie, but his dad finally called up to him after waking up.

David had been knocked out. He woke up with a broken back, a shattered arm, a crushed heel, and a long gash in his leg that went down to the bone. David was a bloody and painful mess. Charlie was doing his best not to panic. David told him to lower him 20 feet down to a ledge he saw below him.

Charlie then had to lower the backpack with the first aid kit inside. Once David had wrapped his leg, he told Charlie to climb down to his ledge. They were a long way from anyone who could help them. Before they could even think about that, they had to get off the face of that mountain. It wouldn't be easy with all of David's injuries.

Charlie would have to lower his dad down the mountain. The process involved Charlie lowering his dad half the length of the rope. Then he would lower himself down. David would then hammer in a new anchor into the wall of the mountain with one hand, and Charlie would pull the rope down, work it through the new anchor and do it all again. David nearly passed out from the pain several times. They'd be in really big trouble if he passed out. Charlie wouldn't be able to get down without his dad's help.

It took the rest of the day, but they finally made it down the huge cliff. The sun was setting and it was getting cold. David was wearing shorts and a t-shirt. Their camp was a mile away. Charlie ran across the boulders and rocks to get there. He grabbed sleeping bags, warm clothes, and food. He filtered water from the lake and packed that, too.

David was shivering badly as he watched the light from Charlie's headlamp making its way through the darkness back to him. They got David into warmer clothes and his sleeping bag. Charlie made him eat and drink. He would just sleep for minutes at a time and kept checking on his dad throughout the cold night, lying there in the boulder field. Hopefully no more boulders would fall on them that night.

David was in so much pain he couldn't sleep. The odds of surviving this were anyone's guess, he thought. But Charlie was brave and he had to make it for him. Fortunately, David was alert the next day. It would be just as difficult getting to their camp as it had been getting off the mountain. Crawling over boulders in his condition was extremely difficult. He blacked out numerous times and left a trail of blood behind him. He had Charlie encouraging him the whole way and scouting for the best way to go.

After all day of painful crawling, the pair finally made it to their camp. David washed his leg wound in the lake. Charlie was starving, but David couldn't eat much. The pain was almost unbearable. Charlie was not excited about having to leave his dad to get help. He was terrified that this might be the last time he would see his dad alive. He held him all night long as he slept.

As soon as the sun rose, Charlie headed out. He had 12 miles to cover through mountain lion and grizzly bear territory...by himself. But his dad's life hung in the balance. If he failed, his dad was a dead man. Charlie told his dad to keep an eye out for the helicopter that he would send, gathered his courage, and set out on the trail.

He had been three miles, blowing his whistle to scare off bears. He prayed continuously as he went. This trail was a tough one. It had gotten steep. Were those voices he just heard? It was! Charlie sees a man and his 19 year old son. They wondered if they should go to David or help make sure Charlie finds the help he's looking for. Charlie insists that they go help his dad. They agree.

Charlie continues a few more miles and he hears voices again. It's a family with one of their friends. That friend used to serve as a Marine. He tells Charlie that he'll run the nine miles all the way to where there should be a park ranger. Charlie will go, too. The former marine runs on ahead.

He got there pretty quick for such a difficult nine mile trail run. The situation demanded it. The Park Rangers jumped into action as soon as they heard someone needed help. Eventually, David was loaded safely into a helicopter...just as Charlie promised.

Keys to Survival: The two days after the accident were incredibly difficult. They required a tremendous amount of determination. The father and son took it a little at a time, but the work wasn't done for Charlie. He did well to make noise to frighten off bears and mountain lions on his rescue hike. His father told him to remember one thing. Stay calm. There was a lot to be afraid of, but by staying calm, Charlie kept going. He was a hero throughout this crazy survival story.

"My name is Shackleton."

This is considered by many to be the most legendary survival story of all time. It is as remarkable as it is improbable. Twenty-six men survived for 625 days (almost two years), trapped in the deadly landscape of the Antarctic ice. Their leader was the man whose name is now forever tied to the meaning of the word "survival". He was Sir Ernest Shackleton, and he managed to keep every single one of his men alive.

Ernest's father was a doctor and really tried to get his son to be one as well. But Ernest knew that he was an explorer and joined the navy at 16 years old. He had already made two attempts to reach the South Pole before his ill fated trip leading the ship, the Endurance. One explorer was already the first to reach the south pole, so Ernest's plan was to walk all the way across Antarctica. That would be 1800 miles in the most unforgiving terrain in the world. Ernest wasn't interested in easy. He needed a bold challenge.

World War I was breaking out in Europe when he departed on his mission. In three months, the Endurance reached the final port before Antarctica. This was the island of South Georgia. It was remote, mountainous, and usually covered in snow. It was a whaling base for England in a most inhospitable place. It is about halfway between South America and

Antarctica. Ernest and his crew left that island for the 1,200 mile journey to Antarctica in December of 1914.

After only two days of sailing, they got slowed by sea ice. They would have to sail through ice the rest of the way and use their ship as a battering ram. After more than a month at sea, they sailed into some very densely packed ice. They decided to wait for an opening. This decision led to disaster. By morning, the ice had hardened all around the boat. They were now trapped in a huge, floating island of ice.

The Endurance would now go where the ice island went and it was floating north across Antarctica's Weddell Sea, away from where Ernest had wanted to go. But the men had no choice but to make the best of things. They built igloos for their sled dogs. They played soccer on the ice. They lived on that drifting ice for nine months. Finally, the ice crushed their ship forcing the men off of it.

Ernest knew this would eventually happen. When they first realized they were trapped, he told the ship's captain (Frank Worsley) that, "what the ice gets, the ice keeps." He didn't expect them to have as long as they did on the boat before it was finally destroyed.

They were now living on a five foot deep block of ice. They only had lightweight tents that they could see the moon through. There was less protection from the wind out on the ice. They eventually ran out of food, so they hunted seals and penguins. For a time, hunting was plentiful, but it wouldn't last. They loved the 69 sled dogs that they had with them but were forced to eat them over the months that followed. The ice got thinner and thinner. They no longer had a ship and their ice island would not stay together for much longer.

They did have three lifeboats that they had saved. It was a good thing they did. They eventually had to sail off the ice that had been their home for more than a year. It was a brutal journey to get to land in the little boats. Freezing water sprayed them constantly in the high seas. After seven days of agonizing work, they made it to the desolate and rocky Elephant Island, just off the coast of Antarctica.

The captain, Frank Worsley, had not slept for 80 hours when they finally made it. It was an extremely dangerous journey. Another of Ernest's officers later wrote, "at least half the party were insane." But they were finally on dry land for the first time in sixteen months.

Now they had new problems. Ships didn't sail past Elephant Island. Nobody knew where they were. After resting up, Ernest, Captain Worsley, and four of the men, set off to go 800 miles back to South Georgia Island in one of the lifeboats. The lives of the 22 men who were left on Elephant Island depend completely on the success of Ernest making it and then coming back on a larger boat to rescue them. This would be Ernest's biggest challenge yet.

Ernest only packed two and a half weeks worth of food. If they were still at sea after that time, it would mean that they had missed South Georgia Island. That meant death. There were no landmarks out there.

Frank Worsley had to navigate with only his handheld instruments. South Georgia Island wasn't small, but it was out in the middle of the ocean. It would be extremely easy to miss. The men sailed across hundreds of miles for an incredible 16 days in the little lifeboat.

As they were nearing their destination, Ernest saw some clouds in the distance. But then he realized that he wasn't looking at clouds. It was a giant rogue wave. He described it this way, "During twenty-six years' experience of the ocean in all its moods I had not encountered a wave so gigantic." Terrifying!

The small lifeboat with six brave souls onboard, went up and up and up with the wave. Miraculously they did not flip or sink. The boat filled up halfway with freezing water that had to be bailed out with desperation. They fought for their lives during and after surviving that wave. They encountered hurricane force winds, and STILL they made it to land! This 800 mile journey by these six men, is still to this day considered the greatest accomplishment in seafaring history. Their success was completely unlikely, but their work was not done.

They had landed on the opposite side of South Georgia Island from the whaling base. Ernest, Frank Worsley, and another man would have to hike more than 20 miles to the other side of the island. In between, was a deadly passage over glaciers and mountains. No one had ever crossed this island here before.

They pushed screws they took from the lifeboat through the soles of their boots to give them grip on the ice. They took a little food and had 50 feet of rope. More than 40 years later, their path would be re-traced by explorers who were amazed that Ernest was able to pull it off. They said, "I do not know how they did it, except that they had to."

Ernest did have to. He would not be stopped now. He still had 22 men to save. It took them 36 hours of nonstop marching across snow covered mountains to reach the whaling station. Imagine the whalers' shock when three men came stumbling up to them. It would be similar to an astronaut on the moon seeing three men walk up out of nowhere.

The station manager managed to croak out an incredulous, "Who the (heck) are *you*?" The man in the middle of the three said, "My name is Shackleton." One whaler was so stunned when he heard that, he started to cry. They sent a boat around to collect the three remaining men on the other side of the island.

Now rescue efforts for the 22 men still stuck on Elephant Island began. Meanwhile, each day the men prepared for rescue in case that day was the day that their leader returned to save them. But as the months dragged on, many of them had lost hope. They were not still waiting for rescue because Ernest was being lazy. He had tried three times to rescue them! And each time, ice had made it impossible to reach them, forcing the rescue ship to go back.

Finally, the men saw a boat. Ernest had been gone for 128 days. He was overjoyed as he approached that he counted all 22 men still there. The men all happily climbed aboard and were reunited. Their nearly two year long icy nightmare was finally over.

Abandoned on a Deserted Island...
for FOUR YEARS!

Long ago, in the year 1676, one of the world's great rascals was born in a small Scottish fishing village. His name was Alexander Selcraig. This unruly scamp was a troublemaker from the start. He got in trouble as a kid for "indecent conduct in church", but on his court date, he was missing. He had escaped to the sea. He spent a lot of time out on the ocean.

He would eventually leave his little town for good after he got in a fight with his brothers, his father, and even one of his brother's wives. Alexander was fighting everyone! This guy had a real problem getting along with people. He'd show them! He changed his last name to Selkirk and left for good. He would spend the rest of his life as a pirate.

He joined up with one of history's famous pirates, William Dampier, who was the first known person to sail all the way around the world three times. The English went to war with Spain around this time and recruited pirates to attack the Spanish. Pirating was now legal as long as they attacked the right boats. After a few years, Alexander ended up on a boat captained by Thomas Stradling. The crew didn't like Thomas. This meant that our quarrelsome hero, Alexander, definitely didn't like him.

The crew had sailed to the island, Màs a Tierra, which is more than 400 miles off the coast of Chile. No people lived there. It's way out in the South Pacific Ocean. It's a big, mountainous island of 35 square miles. The crew was there for a month and on the verge of mutiny. Alexander felt that their ship wasn't seaworthy. He got into a big argument with his captain and told him that he wasn't getting back on the boat. He had assumed that the rest of the crew would join him, but none of the men joined Alexander.

Thomas was excited for his chance to be rid of him. He left the angry Alexander a gun, a knife, a hatchet, a bible, a pot, and some clothes. No food. As soon as Alexander realized that nobody was joining him, his anger turned to fear and regret. He begged Thomas to let him back on the boat. But Thomas wanted no part of it and sailed off, leaving Alexander behind, now a castaway. Time would justify Alexander's doubts about their ship, when it sank and most of the men died. Thomas was carried off to a Spanish prison.

The reality of Alexander's situation must have started to settle in as the pirate ship disappeared over the horizon leaving him utterly alone (except for the hundreds of bellowing sea lions, of course). There were lots of animals on this island which was a good thing. The weather was good so that helped, too. Alexander fished and caught lobsters to eat. Eventually, he had to move away from the coast because the sea lions would chase him off and even Alexander knew better than to get into a fight with those things.

When he went inland, he found freshwater springs and lots of food there. There were cabbage trees, berries, and turnips growing, as well as lots of goats. The goats had gotten there off of other boats and the population had really grown. Alexander had an easy time hunting them.

Alexander built a couple of huts to live in and got quite comfortable. But even then, he would be attacked by rats at night. Fortunately, there were also cats on the island. He became friendly with them and brought several who came to trust him to live in his hut. He never had trouble from the rats again.

What plagued Alexander the most was loneliness, but eventually he got more and more at ease with solitude. Early on, he didn't expect to be on the island for long. The only boats that appeared for years were Spanish boats. They would know him as an enemy pirate and take him prisoner if they found him. He was chased once but because he knew the island so much better than his hunters, he easily escaped. Another time he climbed a tree when he heard voices. It was Spanish soldiers who walked right under him.

Weeks turned into months which turned into years. Alexander had to make new clothes out of goat skins. His hair and beard grew really long and his feet had hardened so he no longer needed shoes. Still, he continuously kept an eye out for ships that might rescue him. After four years and four months of living by himself, he was thrilled to see a British ship! It was a pirate ship like the ones that he had served on.

He probably gave the landing party quite the fright when they saw him. They said that he hardly looked human and had even forgotten how to talk after so long without needing language. Alexander fed them some goat meat and was able to communicate some of his story. Back on the ship was his old pirate captain, William Dampier, who recognized him under all of his hair and goat skins. Alexander joyfully joined the crew and they stayed at sea for another two years, successfully raiding Spanish ships. They finally returned to London, making Alexander's trip an eight year journey.

After a few years, the famous book, *Robinson Crusoe*, was written. It was about a lone shipwrecked survivor who lived on an island by himself. It was based on Alexander's experience and made him famous. Chile even renamed Alexander's island, Robinson Crusoe Island in 1966. Now it is no longer uninhabited but a destination for tourists who want to see the place for themselves.

Keys to Survival: Fortunately, Alexander was a castaway on an island that was teeming with food and drinkable water. To survive for as long as he did, took an incredible amount of willpower. The loneliness would be very difficult to endure. When he was finally found, the once fiery man seemed happy. He had adapted to the solitude and finally found peace. Maybe it's because there was nobody else around for him to argue with.

YOUR REVIEW

What if I told you that just one minute out of your life could bring joy and jubilation to everyone working at a kids book company?

What am I yapping about? I'm talking about leaving this book a review.

I promise you, we take them **VERY seriously**. Don't believe me?

Each time right after someone just like you leaves this book a review, a little siren goes off right here in our office. And when it does we all pump our fists with pure happiness.

A disco ball pops out of the ceiling, flashing lights come on...it's party time!

Roger, our marketing guy, always and I mean always, starts flossing like a crazy person and keeps it up for awhile. He's pretty good at it. (It's a silly dance he does, not cleaning his teeth)

Sarah, our office manager, runs outside and gives everyone up and down the street high fives. She's always out of breath when she comes back but it's worth it!

Our editors work up in the loft and when they hear the review siren, they all jump into the swirly slide and ride down into a giant pit of marshmallows where they roll around and make marshmallow angels. (It's a little weird, but tons of fun)

So reviews are a pretty big deal for us.

It means a lot and helps others just like you who also might enjoy this book, find it too.

You're the best!

From all of us goofballs at Big Dreams Kids Books